Come on People Let's Get in the Game

Minority Homeownership is the Key to Financial Stability

By

Davian Clifton

"The Mortgage Therapist"

ACKNOWLEDGMENTS

I would like to first give honor to my Lord and Savior Jesus Christ. Thank you for blessing me with the ability to share the experiences that I have learned from so that someone else may benefit from them. I ask that you allow this book to be placed in front of everyone who may need the information inside of it. I would like to thank my family for allowing me to pen this book instead of spending time with you. I realize I can be a recluse at times especially when I am writing. For that I want to apologize but know that I love each and every one of you more than life itself.

This book has been a long time coming and I am truly excited about the possibilities that may come from this book. I hope that everyone who reads this get everything out of this book which can allow you to obtain The American Dream of homeownership.

Introduction

As I sit down to write this manuscript, our country is currently in an economic crisis. Foreclosures are happening at a record pace, gas prices are higher than ever before, and we sit on the crest of a recession.

I look back over the past 15 years of working in the financial services industry, with 10 of those years in the mortgage business, and I think of all of the people I have assisted in one way or another. I was either convincing them to purchase some needed life insurance to provide security for their loved ones or I was helping them access the equity in their homes in order to pay off some bills, make home improvements, or pay for a child's college education. The main thing that sticks out in my mind is the fact there were not a lot of minorities purchasing homes for the first time.

We are currently in a historic time for our country where an African-American man has taken the oath for the office of the Presidency of the United States of America for the second time. This is an indication of how far our country has evolved. It was over 140 years ago that blacks were able to legally vote and now we have our first minority as president. This should be a barometer of all of the advances for minorities but in actuality, it is not.

We are still dealing with division amongst the races in this country as well. The George Zimmerman murder trial is a representation of that. Mr. Zimmerman was on trial for the murder of 17-year-old Trayvon Martin. The trial separated the country because a white man, Mr.

Zimmerman, shot and killed a black boy, Trayvon Martin. When the verdict came back as Not Guilty, the country was outraged with protests from coast to coast. This is an indication of where we are in America. There is a great divide amongst the races both socially and economically. In this book, I want to focus on the financial divide.

Come on people, let's get in the game. I am referring to my minority brothers and sisters. It is time for us to stop watching the game and get on the field of play. The field of play that I am referring to is the game of homeownership. I am not going to bore you with a bunch of statistics but let me give you this one. Minorities, mainly blacks and Hispanics, are 25% less likely to own a home than our white counterparts are.

Now the reason this is a startling statistic is that we are more likely to spend our money on clothes and automobiles than our white brethren are. Again, the reason this is significant is that our clothes and cars do not help us build wealth. In fact, as soon as we purchase these items we have lost money. Your car depreciates in value and is worth less than you paid, the moment you drive off the car lot. The main reason to focus on homeownership is that in our country this is the most common way to obtain, build, and sustain wealth. Minorities need wealth in order to gain equality in this country.

An old white man once told me that in order for the black man to receive equal treatment from the white man he must position himself where he does not need the white man. He stated that as long as the white man has to provide jobs and financial assistance to the black man he would never look at us as equals. He also stated that it is similar to how a parent looks at a child. As long as the parent is taking care of that child, he will never look at the child as an equal. Now that was a very profound statement but it also had a lot of truth to it.

The twentieth-century "Black Moses," Marcus Garvey, suggested:

> *"There is no force like success, and that is why the individual makes all efforts to surround himself throughout life with the evidence of it. As of the individual, so should it be of the race. The glittering success of Rockefeller makes him a power to the American nation; the success of Henry Ford suggests him as an object of universal respect. The black man must be up and doing if he will break down the prejudice of the rest of the world. We must strike out for ourselves in the course of material achievement, and by our own effort and energy present to the world those forces by which the progress of man is judged."*

We have to stop blaming others for our problems. Now I do realize that we are playing a game of cards with a loaded deck but we do have some opportunities at times that can level the playing field. The main opportunity again that I am referring to is homeownership. Owning a home is the best financial decision, anyone, especially a minority, can ever make. I know that there are some situations that may prevent you from taking that step but for the most part, we all should at least be moving in that direction.

The purpose of this book is to educate and mobilize minorities, mainly African-Americans, Hispanics, and anyone who does not own a home, to move into the ranks of homeownership to establish themselves financially. One of the main reasons for inequalities and injustices in this country is due to the racial gap in wealth, i.e. assets, including property. This gap in wealth is more enduring than the gap in incomes.

Thomas Shapiro, co-author of the book "Black Wealth/White Wealth," wrote that the gap in wealth, which is a 10-fold ratio, is exemplified by what he has termed "transformative assets." A transformative asset is a gift by a parent or other that works to lift a succeeding generation economically and socially beyond his or her own achievements.

In other words, this is when daddy gives or lends his child the down payment to purchase a house that places the child in a position to obtain wealth. In the minority community, we are not usually in position to make such offers to our children.

Most minorities often seem cut off from the economic mainstream. They face higher risks of poverty, joblessness, and incarceration than their fellow citizens do. Community organizing, civil rights legislation, landmark court decisions, and rising education have advanced the cause of racial equality. Overt bigotry has been banished from public places, and polls show that whites harbor fewer prejudices than they used to. However, these improvements have not been enough.

Wealth is the sum of the important assets a person or family owns -- home equity, pension funds, savings accounts, and investments. Wealth is better than income because it is durable. People use income to meet daily expenses, whereas wealth accumulates. People who have wealth tap into it only to deal with emergencies or to take advantage of opportunities - opportunities that usually build more wealth.

Wealth passes down from generation to generation. The main reason African Americans are currently worse off than whites, according to Shapiro, is that today's African Americans inherited less wealth from their parents than today's whites did. It is not hard to see why. The generation of African Americans now passing away, accumulated less wealth because of discrimination in their day that kept most of them poor and denied them opportunities other Americans enjoyed.

The disparity in wealth not only persists, it mushrooms. Without a cushion of inherited wealth, emergencies hit harder, and people who have no nest egg have to let opportunities pass by. Because of the wealth deficit, African Americans, as well as most minorities, find themselves more vulnerable to shocks and less able to capitalize on breaks than whites with the same income. Therefore, the next generation will inherit less, too. The wealth gap will not close anytime soon unless we take action and do something about it.

This book is divided into four components: **Been There Done That, Preparing the Game Plan, Game Time, and lastly Becoming a Player.**

The first part will discuss the lifestyles of most minorities. It will detail the struggles we go through on a daily basis just to survive. It will discuss how the majority of our lives are spent in survival mode, which hinders us from being able to plan our future. The author will share personal experiences in order to allow you to realize that he has been there and done that.

The second part will lay out a game plan. We will discuss the necessary ingredients that we need to repair our financial situations such as bank accounts, fixing our credit, and primarily, establishing a budget. We have to realize that just because there may not be a lot of income or resources available, we still can purchase a home and begin the road to financial stability.

The third part is game time. We will go over the step-by-step moves in order to make this happen. We will discuss how to obtain a pre-approval from a loan officer. We will determine how much house you can afford. I will show you how to go about finding the house that is for you. We will discuss all of the expected costs that you as the buyer will be responsible for. We will also plan for the future, which is something that we usually do not have time to worry ourselves about.

The last section is becoming a player in the game. This section will discuss the opportunities that are now available to you as homeowners that were never accessible before. It will discuss the tax advantages that come with having a mortgage. You think the Earned Income Credit is good? You wait and see how nice that tax return check looks when you have interest payments to deduct from your taxes. It will also introduce you to something that can possibly change your life, equity.

When a homeowner accesses their equity it can be used for so many productive things such as consolidation of bills, home improvements, college education, purchasing investment properties, and so much more. This is when people are able to solidify themselves financially.

Now this is not a book on buying your "dream" home or some tricks you can use. This book will be more than a "how to buy a house" book. It will discuss the financial struggles and poor decisions that are common in our community. It will relate to the situations that we sometimes find ourselves caught in. It will not chastise you or degrade you but empathize with you and assist you in laying out a plan to move toward the first and necessary step to financial stability.

The author comes from a background that only someone from our community can understand. He knows how to "survive" from paycheck to paycheck or better yet from day to day. He understands that we did not choose to be in the financial situation that we are in but he will show you how to change your situation. This is not a dream of riches book but a very down to earth laying it all on the line type of book.

Now although I mentioned blacks and Hispanics as the minorities for this subject, anyone who has not purchased a home is actually in this minority. This is why it is called the American Dream. Owning a home is the foundation to our way of life. If you first secure your home then you can build from that point but so many think that they cannot obtain that dream because of their backgrounds.

I promise you that no matter where you come from or where you are currently at, everyone can be a homeowner. Everyone can have the feeling of walking across the threshold of a home that they own, but we first must take hold of our own destiny.

Frederick Douglas, the ex-slave and famous orator, once said: *"Our destiny is largely in our own hands. If we find, we shall have to seek. If we succeed in the race for life, it must be by our own energies, and our own exertions. Others may clear the road but we must go forward or be left behind in the race for life. If we remain poor and dependent, the wealth of others will not avail us. If we are ignorant, the intelligence of others will do but little for us. If we are foolish, the wisdom of others will not guide us. If we are wasteful of our time and money, the economy of others will only make our destitution the more disgraceful."*

So in other words, ***"Come on People let's Get in the Game."***

PART ONE

Been There, Done That

"My people are destroyed for lack of knowledge;"

Hosea 4:6

I look back nearly fifteen years ago and think of how I got into the financial services business. I can tell you one thing for sure and that is I did not plan to be an insurance agent and later a mortgage loan officer. I graduated college with a degree in speech pathology. Now do not ask me how that happened either.

I remember transferring from the University of Virginia to Hampton University. Well, let us be honest, I had flunked out of the University of Virginia because I never went to class. My roommate and I thought we had perfected the plan of only going to class for midterm and final exams. We would get up in the morning and go to breakfast since we were football players and we had to sign in for every meal at the dining hall.

I always thought it was funny how the football coaches thought it was necessary to require us to sign in at the dining hall to make sure that we ate every meal but they never considered making sure, we went to class. Anyway, we worked our system for an entire year and actually, we did not fail any classes. We both finished the year with a 1.0 grade point average that put both of us on academic suspension.

Well I decided to go home and get a job. I had a daughter at home that needed to support so I figured that I would just go home and start working at the shipyard. I remember sitting in my coach's office for the last time at Virginia and he asked me what it was that I wanted to do with my life. I told him that I would be satisfied with going home and working at the shipyard. Now he did not knock the shipyard but he looked at me and said, "Son you need to get a bigger goal for your life."

You have to understand that was all that I knew. I was the first in my family to go to college. Well my oldest sister went for a year, but then she got married and had a son so she had to work to help pay the bills. Her husband was not making enough to do it on his own. Therefore, all we knew was get a job and if you married someone then we work together to make it happen.

I can remember my parents both going to work every day. We started in the public housing projects but with my mother's insistence, we moved to a house that we rented. We were not poor but I knew that money was tight. My dad always had a "hustle" of some kind on the side. He used to tell me that a man always has to "get his hustle on" just to make ends meet. That meant that if you do not make enough on your job, which was always the case, then you have to find a way to make some extra money. Many times that hustle was not always something legal.

My father worked at a company that made doors and windows. He used to steal the doors from the company and sell them from the house. Now someone reading this might say that he was not setting a great example for his children, but what my father was doing was making a way for his family to survive, which in actuality was setting a good example for his children. If your moral stance on life forces you to believe differently, then so be it.

After I left the University of Virginia, I received several offers from local schools to play ball for them. Back then the NCAA only required that you sit out a year of football in order to transfer schools. I was a decent football player so receiving another football scholarship offer was not that difficult. I can remember sitting at home one summer afternoon and hearing the doorbell ring. It was an old friend of mine who I had played football with at UVA, he had the football coach from Hampton University with him, and he offered me a scholarship on the spot.

I was planning on working at the shipyard but my mother insisted that I finished school. Hampton was only twenty minutes from home so it would actually work out fine. Therefore, I decided to take his offer.

When I transferred to Hampton University I had no idea what I was going to major in since I had not even thought about it while at UVA. I was hanging out with some of the football players and we walked into this office. It was the office of one of the football boosters, who happened to be the Director of Communication Disorders, Dr. Robert Screen. This man was a very successful person who would make a lasting impression on me. He was considered one of the top people in his field in the country. He had offers to head the speech pathology departments at some of the most prestigious universities in the country but he'd decided to stay at Hampton University because it was his alma mater.

This man asked me what I was going to major in and I just threw out public speaking. I really did not plan to major in that but I did not want to seem undecided. He asked me to take a course in his department just to see what I thought about it. Some of the other football players were taking the course so I thought it was a "bird" course and signed up for it. Well that led to me not only majoring in Speech Pathology but also obtaining a bachelor's degree in it. I do not want to toot my own horn but I was proud of graduating because there were 28 seniors on the football team my last year and only three of us graduated. The rest just left school after their eligibility was completed and went home to start working.

The other reason I was proud of graduating was due to something that occurred in a class during my senior year. It was in a departmental course and there were only about 17 or so seniors in our department. Our department was a really close-knit group. The students and the professors had a good relationship. I have stated on many occasions that one of the reasons I was able to finish school was due to feeling obligated not to disappoint my professors. They always showed a genuine desire for everyone to succeed which had an enormous effect on me. I have come to find out that that is a common feeling amongst students of HBCU's (Historically Black Colleges and Universities).

Anyway, a couple of my fellow classmates decided to put together a list of what they felt each individual in our class would be doing ten years from that point in time. They had one of our classmates as the head of a speech pathology department for a major university. Another classmate was a successful professor in our field who had made some very important discoveries in the field of speech. Others were successful business people and even one who had her own talk show. Now we come to my name on the list, and they have me working at a gas station pumping gas. Everyone in the class got a huge laugh out of it so of course I had to come back with the remark of, "If I am pumping gas then I probably own the gas station."

Now as trivial, as that list was it really punched me in the gut. My professor saw that it bothered me and called for me after the class. She asked me for my reaction to the list and I told her that I was pissed off. I immediately defended myself and attacked the characters of the people who created the list. She sat there and listened to me rant and rave about how wrong they were for writing that then she quietly asked me, "So what are you going to do about it?" That question haunted me for years as I went through life trying to find out who I was and what I wanted to do.

I gave professional football a shot and realized that was not going to be my route to success so I moved on. After working in the school system for about a year and coming to the conclusion that I could not take care of my family on that salary, I started looking for other jobs and hustles. I did some of everything from network marketing to newspaper routes.

Now after a couple of years of bouncing from business to business, I was at a guy's house when he was discussing yet another network marketing business. Now do not get me wrong, I am a strong advocate for network marketing businesses. I learned a lot about business and just being a man through my experiences with network marketing.

It exposed me to another life. It allowed me to actually realize that there is another world available for my family and me. I was introduced to real life millionaires and at that point, in my life, I had never met someone who was considered a millionaire. A couple of the guys from football had made it to the pros but that was it. I saw wives who looked at their husbands as if they hung the moon. I had never seen that before. The only look my mother gave my father was the stare of hatred and disgust.

After I sat through the business presentation at this man's house, and it was a beautiful house, I expressed to him that I had been in a similar business before and that I was looking for something different at that time in my life. He was very polite and thanked me for coming. He walked me to my car and while we were talking, he mentioned that he was going to take a class starting the next day to obtain his life insurance license.

Now it had only been a week earlier that I met a guy selling cell phones who was an insurance agent. He came over to my father's house and signed him up for a policy. While I was walking him to his car I asked him how much money he made selling insurance and what he told me really blew my mind because this guy was not the sharpest guy in the world. Therefore, I immediately told myself that if that joker can make that kind of money I knew I would make a mint. So after inquiring about the class some more, I ended up taking the class with him. That class led to me selling insurance for about five years.

I'm not going to sit here and tell you that it was an instant success story. That after getting my license I made a million dollars in my first year. I did not make a million dollars and barely made a thousand dollars, well at least it seemed that way. I enjoyed selling insurance. It came naturally to me because I enjoy talking with people. I was able to make a living but at first that was all I did.

I sold insurance for a few years. Some years were better than others were. One year we got a deal with the state selling critical care insurance to the state employees. That worked out really well and we made some good money that year. We were very excited about the upcoming year and the income potential but as soon as the contract came up for renewal we were told that a more experienced group of insurance agents were awarded the business. See what happened was we took what was perceived as a bottom level opportunity and made it work. When upper level management saw the true income potential in the business they decided that it was too much money for us to handle and they went around us to their contacts at the state level and arranged for the contract to go to someone else.

We were responsible for setting up that contract in the beginning. My partner knew someone who had worked a similar contract in another state. He had a contact at the state level that we used to obtain the contract. Now when we were setting up this deal no one was interested in the business at the upper management levels because we were a group of minority agents who had not really made any significant business production. However, after they saw the production we submitted while working the contract, we got their attention.

The only problem was instead of them helping us manage the business production they found a way to take it away from us. That was a hard pill to swallow because we worked hard arranging that contract. So there I was back at just finding a way to make a living.

While I was attempting to make a living, we were struggling to get by. It seemed as though I was always waiting on a check and by the time the check got there, it was already spent. My wife has always worked and contributed to the household but it always seemed as though we never had enough to pay the bills.

It seemed as though I was always trying to keep something from being turned off whether it was the light bill, gas bill, paying the rent, or keeping the car from being repossessed. It was a never-ending struggle. It is funny now but that was our life for a long time. Actually, that is the life for most minorities in this country. We find a way to make it work. Sometimes it gets a little hard but you just make it through.

I know I have had everything that can be turned off turned off at one time or another. We have sat in the dark waiting to get the money to have the lights turned back on. We have lived in the house with no hot water, having to heat the water on the stove in order to take a warm bath in the sink. We have worn coats to bed because the heat had been turned off and we were trying to stay warm.

I can remember a time when the water was turned off. I would wait for my neighbor to leave for work and go outside with a bucket to borrow, let us be honest, steal, water from his outside faucet just to flush the toilets in our house. I remember wondering what I would say if he caught me stealing the water. He would have let me have the water if I had asked him, but I was too ashamed to admit that I could not pay my water bill.

I can remember a time when I bought a truck in someone else's name because my credit was too bad to get it in my own name. I had been making the payments on time for nearly a year only to find out that the person who had signed for the truck had actually used someone else's information. Therefore, when that person found out that their name had been used to purchase several vehicles they immediately reported them as fraud.

My wife had the truck one day and the repo man was sitting outside of our house. When she pulled into the neighborhood, she saw the tow truck and decided to go to her sister's house instead and call me. Well the repo man saw her in the truck and followed her to her sister's house. When she went inside, he snatched the truck. Now my wife did not know that I had used someone else's credit to get the loan so she thought I had not been making the payments. The main problem was not that the truck was taken; it was that I had been making the payments of $550 a month for nearly a year and now I had nothing to show for it.

I remember sitting in the bankruptcy lawyer's chair on three separate occasions unable to file each time. The first time I went to file for bankruptcy, I realized that I did not have enough money. That was depressing realizing that I could not even afford to file bankruptcy. The second time was halted when I realized that if I filed bankruptcy it could probably cause me to lose my job with the particular insurance agency I was working with. They really looked into an agent's credit history. The last time I went to file, I was sitting in front of an arrogant lawyer who kept making smart remarks about people filing for bankruptcy were using it as an "escape clause" and leaving their debts for the taxpayers to pay. He was really ticking me off so by the time it came for me to sign the initial papers I just got up and left his office. I was determined to pay off my debts and get my credit right on my own. I think that was his plan all the time.

It seemed as though there was always something happening though. Whether it was my paycheck was wrong or did not come or when the direct deposit was made into my checking account the account was so overdrawn that it took the majority of my money. So here I am on payday and still broke. That was a painful feeling knowing that I would not get any more money until the next paycheck.

I can remember using my sister's food stamps in order to bring some food into the house. I can remember being so frustrated one day when the gas man came to shut off our gas that I just snapped and began screaming and threatening the guy. I scared him so badly that he actually left and they did not turn off the gas for another four days, giving me enough time to get the money and pay the bill. I felt bad about that afterwards but at the time, I did what I had to do.

I know how it is not to be able to do the little things for your children like give them lunch money or ride past the convenience store because you do not have any money to buy them some ice cream. That is a hard pill to swallow for anyone, especially a man. I mean it is hard enough to handle the responsibilities of being the so-called "head of the family" but when you cannot provide the basic necessities for your family that messes with a man's mind. That is why some guys just leave their families. They get to a point where they feel the family is better off without them. Now don't get me wrong, I think that is a coward's way of handling it, but I can understand.

Money struggles can dominate a person's thoughts. It is the leading cause for divorce. It can define who you are if you let it. That is why some people cannot even imagine themselves accomplishing certain goals. If they have never seen anyone in their family go to college it is sometimes hard for them to picture themselves going to college. It is like the old saying, "You got to see it to believe it." There is a lot of truth in that.

I can remember I had been a loan officer a few years when I was referred to a young woman. She was in her mid-twenties and had a two-year-old daughter. She had been working at one of the local food processing companies for about five years. She was making decent money but she was living with her mother and wanted me to find her a place to rent. I get many calls similar to this and I always immediately pull their credit to see if I can qualify them for a mortgage. I have always felt it makes more sense to buy than to rent. After pulling her credit, I saw that she had a very good credit score. She always paid her bills on time. I told her that I was going to fill out an application for her for a loan. She immediately told me that she could never buy a house. I told her that was not true and convinced her to fill out the application anyway.

Well to make a long story short, I was able to qualify her for a first time homebuyer's program that would pay 100% of the purchase price. She had been very good with her money and had several thousand dollars saved in the bank. She was still a little skeptical so she asked me to look for a house with her instead of getting a real estate agent. I reluctantly agreed because that is not my thing, but I could see how nervous she was. We were able to find a nice townhouse near a park that she fell in love with. I had a real estate agent friend of mine complete a contract on her behalf and make an offer. The sellers accepted the offer and we moved forward to closing on the house.

A couple of days later I received this message from her that she had changed her mind and was not going to buy the house. She did not give any explanations at all. I attempted to contact her but she would not answer the phone. Then the next day I received another phone call but this was from her mother and she was angry with me. She accused me of taking advantage of her daughter. She said that I had been lying to her about this house and that it was no way in hell her daughter could afford that house. She said that she was going to call the police on me, and the local news station to report on my business practices. She cursed me out every which way she could think of. She called me everything but a child of God.

The call took me off guard so much that I immediately started to laugh which really ticked her off. Then her brother got on the phone and he began to threaten me. Now I am from the streets as well so I do not take kindly to threats. I told him that I was coming over to discuss this with her and the entire family if need be. You see I am from the hood and I know the mindset of the people who live there. The problem was not that this young woman could not afford this house. The problem was that she took her mother to the house and her mother could not believe she could have such a nice house, especially since she was the baby of the family and no one else in the family owned a house. Therefore, I had to have been lying to her about this house.

I went over to her mother's house and just as I expected the house was packed. Now I probably should have taken someone with me but I wasn't worried because I knew I could convince them of the truth in the situation. Even though I was not related to these folks, they were still my people.

The minute I walked in the mother started in on me. I sat there and listened to her concerns. Then the brother said his peace about there was no way his baby sister could afford a house and he had been working for twelve years and did not have a house. Therefore, I had to have been running a scam on her. I sat there and listened to them accuse me of everything from trying to cheat her out of her money to making sexual advances towards her. When they seemed to have finished, I politely asked if I could speak. They both reluctantly nodded in agreement to me.

I explained to them first who I was because I knew it was important for them to know that I was from the same section of town that they were. I told them where I grew up. I told them who my family was and gave them some names. This seemed to surprise the mother because it was obvious that she knew my people once I said their names. I looked at the brother and reminded him of when I had seen him before. He did not realize it but I coached against his son's basketball team a couple of years prior. His entire emotional position changed at that point.

Once I had familiarized myself to them, I focused in on the daughter. I asked the daughter if I had been professional with her the entire time. She replied that I had gone above and beyond with her. I asked her if I have explained to her all of the details of the mortgage including costs that she would have after closing in which she replied yes.

I explained to the family that they should be proud of the fact that she was able to purchase a home. Here she was a single mother in her twenties working everyday and taking good care of her little girl. I told them that not only did she have good credit but also she has been disciplined enough to save a significant amount of money. I told the mother that the daughter told me that she learned to pay her bills and save her money by watching her mother handle her business. I told the mother that her daughter told me how she had raised her four children by herself working two and three jobs. She told me how they never went without and how she even helped her sister raise her children.

Well at this point, the mother was bubbling with pride. She then looked at me with genuine concern and asked me if her daughter could really afford that house. Now they did not know who I was or what I could do. You see I was born to speak to groups. I have no fear of speaking in public. At that point, I took out a legal pad, literally broke down the numbers for them, and showed them how she would be able to pay her bills, have money to live off, as well as put away some money every month. I also showed them that in a few years the amount of equity she should have built up in the house and the things that she could do with it. They did not know what equity was but liked what I said could be done with it.

The problem was that no one in that family had ever lived anywhere but in the projects. Therefore, the thought of buying a house had never entered their minds. They felt that if they were able to get an apartment in the projects that they had become successful in the eyes of their community. I asked the brother what type of work he did and he told me he had been a longshoreman for over twelve years. I told him that I used to scab down at the docks while in college. I mentioned the names of the guys I worked with and of course, he knew all of them, which really gave us a connection. I then asked him why it was that he did not own a home.

He explained that his sister was a single mom with three kids and in order to help her out, he and his fiancée stayed at his sister's apartment with their two-year-old daughter. This really shocked me because a longshoreman in our part of the state makes a significant income. Actually, a longshoreman is one of the highest paid jobs a man can get without a college degree in our community. I asked him where his sister's apartment was located and he told me the name. I mentioned that I had just seen on the news where the police had raided an apartment in that complex the day before. He nodded and added that the apartment belonged to his next-door neighbor. He said that his fiancée and daughter were home and the noise scared his daughter.

I looked at him and shook my head in disgust. I stared him in his eyes and said, "Why the hell are you placing your family in danger like that?" He was shocked that I had spoken to him that way and had a puzzled look on his face. I continued by asking, "What if the police would have had the wrong apartment number and busted down your sister's door? Your daughter would have been playing right in front of the door and could have gotten hurt." I then said to him abruptly, "...and it would have been your fault."

He became upset at that point because he knew that what I was saying was the truth. I told him that it was obvious that he was the head of this family and that the family's protection fell on him. I told him that I noticed the new Escalade ESV with 24-inch rims parked outside. I asked him if it belonged to him. He admitted that it did. I then asked him if it made any sense to park a $70,000 truck outside of an apartment in the projects where it is not even safe enough to let his child go outside to play. I said wouldn't it be better for his family and his sister's family to live in a nice neighborhood where all of the kids could play without everyone having to worry about stray bullets and everything else crazy that happens in the projects?

At that point, every adult in the house was asking me what he or she could do to get a house. They were all patting the young woman on her back telling her how proud they were of her. The problem was that they could not see this young girl owning her own home especially since no one else in the family owned one. They all wanted a home of their own but did not know the process or if it was even possible.

In the minority communities, the perception of what is important has always been screwed up. We are more concerned with our image amongst those who do not matter than we are about what is important. A man's family should come before anyone or anything except God. We should focus on insuring that our children receive the best education and have advantages that we did not receive. Instead, we are focused on what makes us feel good. We feel that because we work a job every day we are "entitled" to certain things.

I can remember my father saying to me that a man should have a good car. If he works everyday, he deserves to drive a nice car. That is what I heard my entire life up until I was about thirty years old. He always said if you want something just go get it and pay whatever for it. You deserve it because you work every day. I believed this for a long time.

I would go and finance a car and did not care how much the payments were going to be. I felt that I worked every day and I deserved to have a good car. It did not matter that the payments were going to be too high and cause me to struggle to pay my other bills. It did not matter that my insurance was going up because of that new car. I just kept telling myself that I deserve to have a new car. It would make me feel better on those days that I could wash my car and ride around in it. Well the problem was that I had to end up working extra hours or even worse getting a second part-time job to pay for the car.

I continued to take my father's advice all the way, until he passed away. That is when reality set in. I realized that my father worked his entire life until he retired on disability and when he died, I had to pay for his funeral. I had been taking financial advice from someone who was broke his entire life. That is the story for many of us. We continue to listen to people who do not have any more than we do. A broke man cannot do anything for another broke man. We should always be careful of who we take advice from. I used to believe that you get what you deserve but in reality, you get what you earn a right to possess.

I remember watching the "Oprah Winfrey" show one day. The episode focused on a woman whose husband had just committed suicide and left her completely broke. They showed how the husband had damaged their credit and ruined her finances. She described how for years they had lived above their means and she never knew how much money they had. Evidently, the pressure became too much for her husband and he shot himself with a gun.

Now the first thing that came to my mind was this is something that you would never, well rarely, see in a minority family. Suicide is very rare with minorities. We are used to struggling through life especially when dealing with money. The fact that we looked up and suddenly realized that we are broke is not a life changing moment for us. It is usually just a Monday morning for us.

The second issue I had with this particular show was that Oprah had Suze Orman, the financial expert, to work with this woman. Suze Orman is a great person. I have heard her speak live at a conference with Donald Trump. I have always watched her on CNN and different shows. I have the upmost respect for her and her accomplishments. The only problem I have with Suze is she does not give advice for those who do not already have resources.

Suze is known for giving "tough love" to people. She is known for telling it like it is. The question I have for Suze is, "Does she know how it really is?" I mean can she really relate to what it feels like being a minority in this country struggling to put food on the table. She discusses what a person should do with their 401(k). If they should place it in a money market account or trust a mutual fund manager? The average person in this country does not have a 401(k) account and could not tell you the difference between a money market account and a public library account.

A great example to my point was Suze had this woman hold an estate sale. The fact that she owned enough personal possessions to have an "estate sale" lets you know that she was not financially ruined. In our community that would have been a yard sale. The only difference was this "estate sale" earned the woman $13,000. If someone in our community has $13,000 they are in pretty good shape whether she had lost her husband or not. Most women are not left with anything after the death of their spouse.

The next thing that Suze did that I thought was interesting was she made this woman's family come together to discuss her situation. She asked the family who would help her get back on her feet. One couple said they could afford to give her $1,000 a month to help her out. Another man said that he would co-sign for an apartment for her while others agreed to do things such as help her move and whatever else she might need.

Now this came as a surprise to me because of the fact that she had to contact the family to get them to help this woman. In our community, family is all that we have. Our families may be considered "dysfunctional" but we have always leaned on each other. It is an understood fact that we will help our family members even when we really should not. That is usually when we get into trouble for co-signing for a relative and they default on the loan.

Suze is great for the average middle class person, those individuals who are probably already homeowners. They have a solid job with a decent income. They have multiple accounts such as checking, savings, 401(k), and mutual funds. They have the option of placing their children in private schools or not. They have options in life.

She does not address those persons who have never owned a home and probably do not have anyone in their family who does either. They have a job but do not make enough to pay the bills. They do not have any accounts especially a checking account because they are scared that someone may find out about it and take their money for one reason or another. They do not have the option of sending their children to private school. They are trying to keep a roof over their heads so that child protective services will not come and take them away. Their options in life are very limited or at least that is how they feel.

Now please do not think that I am anti-Suze Orman. I have watched and listened to her for years and agree with some things and disagree with others. My feelings toward whom she focuses on are just that, my feelings. I still think she does a wonderful job for those she chooses to work with. I just feel that there has come a time for someone to help the real everyday person. Those of us who struggle everyday just to keep our heads above water.

Most minorities truly understand what the word struggle really means. Struggling is not when you have to decide not to take a vacation this year. Struggling is not cutting back on playing golf and having to use the public course instead of the private country club course. Struggling is not when you have to eat hamburger instead of your normal steak for dinner. These are the reasons most people do not listen to the so-called "financial experts." They feel as if they do not understand their life and cannot relate to their struggles.

Struggling is when you are a single mom and you find yourself out in the street and have to decide between going to this shelter or staying with a guy who will let you and your kids stay at his house in exchange for sex.

Struggling is when you are a man and you were just laid off from your job, trying to figure out how to pay the rent, without doing something illegal. so that your family will not be put out in to the streets. Struggling is being a senior citizen living on a fixed income trying to decide between buying food or your medicine.

We have struggled and survived long enough as a group and as a people. It is time that we move into the next phase of our existence. As I stated earlier in this book we will not be accepted as equals in this country until we position ourselves as financial equals. The first step to making this metamorphosis is homeownership.

I used this entire portion of the book to reveal to you my past financial decisions. I wanted to familiarize myself to you and let you know that I have been there and done that. I did that because many people do not want to know what you know until they first know how much you care. That is why I stood naked in front of you revealing everything from my past so that you can realize that I know where you are coming from. Now I need you to listen to me and come along for the ride.

:

PART TWO

Preparing the Game Plan

"God bless the child who's got his own"

Billie Holiday

The previous chapter was used to let you realize that everyone makes bad decisions with their finances. Most of the time we are just doing whatever is necessary to survive. No one wants to struggle financially but sometimes it is what it is. That section was necessary because most people always think that they are the only one who is in the position they are in, but always remember: No Condition is Permanent. Now it is time to develop a game plan to get ourselves in position to purchase that house and establish ourselves financially.

We are going to discuss credit in general and the elusive credit report. We are going to learn how to read it and use it to our advantage. We are also going to discuss the importance of a budget and go over some basic guidelines in setting up a budget for your family. Lastly, we are going to discuss banking decisions. We are going to detail why it is bad business to cash our checks at the local grocery store or that check-cashing place on the corner. We are going to discuss why it is necessary to deal with a reputable banking institution.

Credit

In our country, credit is one of the most important entities in our lives. It comes in many forms starting with credit cards to automobile loans to home mortgages. In some communities, credit can also include what is on the books at the local grocery store or even worse, what is on the books with the local loan shark. No matter how you obtain it or use it, credit can dictate your life.

It can mean the difference between driving a reliable late model vehicle to riding in a "pray every time you turn the key" car. It can mean living in an area where your kids can go outside to play to living where you have to eat dinner on the floor in order to avoid being hit by a stray bullet. It can also mean the difference in getting a good paying job with benefits to having a job asking, "Do you want fries with that?"

Our society is a credit driven society. That is a good thing but it can also be a bad thing. A person can be caught up with this credit thing and find themselves in a lot of debt. I can remember my first year of college. I was only 18 years old and away from home for the first time in my life. On my way to the cafeteria one day, I noticed a flyer that said, "Mail a copy of your Student ID, and get a VISA card." Now at first, I thought it was some trick but I heard one of the guys at lunch say that he got a credit card for $500 by sending in his ID. Well given the fact that I was broker than the Ten Commandments at the time, I could not wait to send in my ID.

It took about two weeks before it came but there it was a brand new VISA card from Citibank. I had never even seen a credit card before. I do not think my mother even had one at the time. Now of course I put it away to use only for emergencies. Yeah right! I could not wait to get to the mall. I think I used that entire $500 in about two weeks after getting it in the mail.

Then the fun began about a month later. I started receiving bills in the mail. The bills were followed by phone calls from Citibank. Now it never occurred to me how I was going to pay for this credit card. I did not have a job and in fact, I could not have a job since I was on an athletic scholarship. I could not get my mother to pay for it because she was having a tough enough time paying her own bills. That thought never entered my mind. I was only focused on buying any and every thing that I could get my hands on.

That little encounter in my life led to a long-term relationship with Citibank. In fact, I think I was about 35 before I finally paid off that credit card. By the time I paid it in full, the total amount came to over $1,500.00. I never told my mother about that credit card either.

That was one of my first adventures with credit. You have to be very careful of what seems to be a good deal. That became evident when my girlfriend and I decided to get married. Neither of our families could afford to pay for a wedding for us so it was on us. We did not have a lot of money so we had to make a decision. It was have both a wedding and honeymoon or go to the justice of the peace to get married; then get an apartment and buy furniture.

As I am sure, you can figure out, we decided to get an apartment and buy furniture. The entire purchase was going on our brand new Discover card. We maxed the card out in a single weekend but took six years to pay it off. By the time we paid off the card we could no longer use the cheap furniture we bought with it.

Credit is good when used wisely. It should never be used to purchase anything on a whim. It should be used for major purchases such as a home or car. You should have a credit card for emergencies. You should never purchase routine items such as groceries, movie tickets, and clothing with your credit card. If you do not want to carry cash then use a debit card that works with your checking account. If you do not have a checking account then do not worry. We will discuss that a little later in this section.

Again, credit is essential in today's society. If you are one of those people who have made up their minds that they do not need credit then you are in for a rude awakening. Your credit is reviewed for so many aspects of your life. I mentioned earlier about employment. They also look at your credit for banking, apartment rentals, insurance, utilities, satellite television, and so much more. I know you have survived this long without it but for the purpose of this book, which is homeownership for financial stability, it is a necessity.

That brings us to the first step in dealing with our credit. We must look at our credit report. Most people have never seen their credit report. I know whenever I meet with a client for the first time and I ask them what is on their credit report they have no idea. Some of them can maybe tell me one of their scores but most do not have any idea what a credit report even looks like. That is because most creditors make it a practice not to allow the customers to see their report. It is a way of keeping people in the blind so to speak, in order to retain a position of control.

If you do not have any idea what your credit situation is, then you cannot negotiate a better deal for yourself. They want to have you think that they are pulling strings just to get you any type of credit because of your score. That might seem a little underhanded but that comes with sales. I always give people a copy of their report so that they can go over it with me. The majority of the time people are surprised at the fact that their credit is not as bad as they thought it was.

There are three main credit bureaus that are used to determine a person's credit rating: Transunion, Experian, and Equifax. When obtaining credit the lender will contact one of the three to find out your credit score. It depends on the type of credit that determines the bureau they normally use.

When attempting to obtain a mortgage loan they use all three bureaus and go by your middle score. For example, if your Transunion score is 650, your Experian is 685, and your Equifax is 700 then your middle score is 685. Some lenders add all three scores together and then divide it by three to get an average score. It is very simple.

Whenever you apply for credit, the lender reports to all three bureaus whether or not you were approved. The lender then reports either monthly or quarterly to the bureaus your payment history. That is whether you have paid them on time, late, or not at all. The bureaus each have a unique scoring method to determine your credit score. Your score can range from 0-850 with 850 being the best. A person with a score above 680 is considered prime or A rating. A person below a 680 is considered sub-prime.

You should take these scores seriously but they are not life or death. People are really hung up over their scores when I tell them, which is funny to me because before they knew what their scores were they did not care about their credit. Now when I tell them they have a lot of work to do on their credit they look like they want to jump off a bridge. Remember this entire credit process is like a game.

Before you can be successful in any game, you need to at least know the rules. We did not make up the rules but we still have to follow the rules in order to be successful at the game. There are those who will tell you they can manipulate the rules in order to short cut the system but what I have learned over the last decade of working in the financial services industry is one thing. You have to pay your bills.

Many times when I go over a person's credit report, they get angry. Therefore, my first response is maybe the items on their report are incorrect because that happens a lot. You get someone with a similar name or close social security number and you are being credited for someone else's credit purchase. However, this is usually not the case; they are upset with the fact that certain creditors actually reported their accounts to the credit bureaus. For some reason they were under the impression that certain creditors would not report them to the credit bureaus. When I verify the information with them, they agree to having the account and not paying it but they were under the understanding that after a certain period it should not be on the report.

Let me address this misconception upfront. Yes, there are times that certain accounts disappear from a person's report. The company may have gone out of business and all of their accounts were written off by a buyout or bankruptcy. Normally an account can stay on your report for seven years from the date of last activity, with court judgments and bankruptcies reporting for ten years.

The thing that most lenders will do is continue to update your account, which changes your date of last activity. In other words, the time clock for the seven-year mark continues to restart. Most of the time though a delinquent account will remain on your report until it is paid and even then you have to request that it be removed. This is my rule of thumb and it took me a long time to accept this fact myself. If you owe the money then pay the money. If someone owed you some money, wouldn't you want him or her to pay you? You would not want them to think that it has been a few years since I borrowed that money from you so I figured that I should not have to pay you now. You would be ready to fight.

Now I know this is not what you want to hear but again I told you in the very beginning of this book that this is not going to be a how to get over type of book. If you are not in position to purchase a home right now, you will just have to have patience and work through the mess that you made until we get there. There is no other way for me to say it other than that. My pastor use to always say, "You didn't create your credit mess overnight so don't expect to fix it overnight." So again, I am only here to tell you the rules of the game and coach you to the finish. The finish line is when you have been in your house for a year after closing, stress-free.

I feel a need to address this topic a little more. Many people come to me asking for my assistance to help them purchase a home. Once I determine that they are not ready and need some work on their credit they get disappointed and just do not try. They succumb to the fact that they are not meant to have a house and just give up. Let me tell you something. It took me over ten years to get myself together before I was able to purchase a home. Ten years! There were many times that I thought it would never happen but I never gave up. I knew that if I just did what I was supposed to do then eventually it would happen.

Remember that God is no respect of person meaning if He blesses someone else He will bless you as well. You just have to put yourself in position to be blessed.

This reminds me of a movie that I love to watch whenever I may be feeling down. It is entitled, "Facing the Giants." It is a true story about a small Christian high school football team in Georgia. The coach had experienced six losing seasons in a row. They were starting a new season and found out that one of their best players had just transferred to another school. The players were down as well as the fans. The coach was beside himself trying to figure out what to do. One day while sitting in his office a man walks in and tells him that the Lord told him to tell the coach that he should stay where he has been planted and continue to work hard. He then tells the coach a story about two farmers. The farmers were both struggling with their farms because they were experiencing a drought. They both had been praying feverishly for rain. Well one farmer just sat around complaining about how bad things were but the other farmer kept preparing his fields for the rain.

One day the Lord opened the skies and poured down the rain onto the farms. The man then asked the coach, "Which farmer do you think benefited from the rain?" The coach replied, "The one who prepared his fields." The man then asked the coach, "Which one are you? Are you the one who is sitting around complaining about how bad things are or are you the one who is preparing himself for a blessing?"

My sister suggested that movie to me during a rough time that I was experiencing. My money was really messed up and the bills were just out of control. It seemed as though everyday just brought a different obstacle for me to try to get over. I was sitting around having a major "pity party." When I saw that movie, especially that part of the movie, I had to ask myself, am I preparing my fields for the rain? I could not honestly answer that question with a yes. All I was doing was complaining about how bad things were. I was not proactively dealing with the situation. I was reactively dealing with the problems.

From that point on, I attacked my situation. I no longer sat around and accepted my situation as my destiny. I decided that if the Lord blessed people who I knew were in the same situation as me then why wouldn't He do the same thing for me. I just had to discipline myself to do what was required to change my predicament and everyone can do the same thing. No one's situation is permanent.

I heard Les Brown say:

*"In order for us to take life on, even in the worst times, we have to say to ourselves that **I am going to make it no matter what**. Not making it is not an option."*

Let us get back to the credit report. The credit report's main purpose is to give the lender an indication of what to expect from you if they lend you the money. I like to give an example to my clients of you receiving a large sum of money. You just received a large inheritance from a long lost uncle you never knew existed. Now that you have money everybody and their brother is coming at you to borrow money. Since you were blessed, you feel obligated to help people out. You do not have so much that you can just give it away but you are willing to loan out some money.

The first potential borrower is your friend of ten years, Jim. You guys used to work together and even played on softball teams together. He has always had a steady job and lived at the same residence for as long as you have known him. You have never heard of Jim having any money problems, in fact, he borrowed some money from your brother one time and actually gave him back more than he borrowed. You feel good about loaning him some money because it is a good chance you will get it back on time plus interest.

The second potential borrower is your cousin, Pookie. Pookie has not had a steady job in over ten years. He has lived with everyone in the family at one time or another and left owing each one some money. Pookie is known around town to owe a lot of people money and now that you think about it he still owes you money from a couple of years back.

So here, you have two applicants who would like to borrow money from you. Jim wants to use the money to purchase some power washing equipment to add to his current landscaping business. Pookie wants to borrow the money to finish a hip-hop CD demo he has been working on for the last five years. He plans to be the first fifty-year old rapper to make it big. Which one are you more comfortable lending money to?

As crazy as I made that sound that is exactly how a lender looks at an application. They first look at your past credit history. Does he pay his bills on time especially his rent? If he has been late before, is it a constant or did something happen? Does he have consistent employment in the same field for at least 3-4 years? Has he resided at the same residence for the past couple of years or does he move around every 6 months? These are some of the items that a lender looks at to determine if they think you will pay them their money back.

It is really that simple. Would you want to lend money to Jim or Pookie? Who do you think is going to pay you your money back and on time? You have to put yourself in a position where people trust you with their money. Once that happens you will have no more worries.

I was talking with my barber one day in the grocery store. I asked him how things were going because I had not seen him in a while. He does not work at the shop everyday anymore. He has been out purchasing real estate. He told me that he had just bought the building next to his shop and was going to make it a billiards room. I thought that was great and being a mortgage broker I immediately asked him who was funding it for him. He told me that a local bank was doing the funding and they had refinanced his barbershop as well.

Now this came to a surprise to me because I remember having talks with him years ago about experiencing some of the same financial struggles that I was going through. We used to compare notes so to speak about our struggles while laughing about them. You might as well laugh then cry. I asked him how he was able to get the bank to finance those deals and he told me that he had been working on his credit for the last several years and got it over 700. He said now the bank calls him to offer money. He said they now refer to him as Mr. Cross. Before that, it was just Travis. Nevertheless, while he was struggling to pay his payments to them it was, "Hey boy, where is my money?" It is funny how you are treated when they know you will pay them their money back.

That is another example of what I mean when I say you have to learn to play the game. You see Travis did not allow his struggles early on to define who he was. I remember him telling me about how he owed everybody he knew at one time or another. You see he could have very easily let that temporary setback in life brand who he was. He could have just gone through life accepting the fact that his financial situation was in shambles and it would probably never get better. Instead, he decided that he was better than that and he would not allow that situation to define him. Now he is walking around enjoying life. He has given himself options which is the basic purpose in this game we call life.

Now that you understand the purpose of having good credit, let us begin working on your credit. Okay we have your credit report in front of you. We have already discussed the score. Let us look at what determines the score. Each bureau has their own formula to determine your credit score and for the life of me, I have never been able to figure it out. I know what factors go into the formula though.

They look at how much credit you have and how much of that has been used. They refer to that as the Credit Utilization Score. For example, you may have a credit card with a limit of $1,000 and a balance of $500. At that point, your ratio is 50%. However, let us say that you also have another credit card with a limit of $1,000 and the balance is $0. Then your ratio is only 25%. That means you are only using a quarter of the entire credit amount that you have access to. The creditors want you to keep that ratio under 35%. That shows the lender that you are not credit hungry. You do not spend every dime that is given to you. Most people are unaware that if their balance is 50% or higher of their limit, they are actually hurting their score, even if they never make a late payment.

Many people think that if they pay off all of their accounts and close them then that will help but actually, it will hurt them. You need open accounts to show a credit history. It is just better to pay down the balances. Now what I normally tell my clients is when you get some extra money like a bonus at work or your income tax return, use that money to work on your credit balances. You can always contact a creditor and negotiate a payment schedule or reduced amount to pay off the debt.

Now that may have lost half of my readers. They are thinking that I must be crazy thinking that they are going to spend their tax return or Christmas bonus money to pay off some bills. That is exactly what I am telling you to do. You have to sacrifice spending to get your debt and credit under control. I know you feel like you deserve to go shopping when this money comes but I am here to tell you that the day you move into your own house you will feel so much better than any shopping spree you have ever had in your life. I can promise you that.

The next thing that affects your credit report is payment history. The creditors look at how often were you late on a payment. They do not expect you never to have any late payments because they understand that life happens and that causes situations at times. They just do not like to see patterns of late payments. Obviously, a 30-

day late is better than a 90-day late. However, even a 90-day late can be explained and worked out. We just want to make sure we are making the majority of payments on time.

If there are several accounts that have consistent late payments, the first thing we are going to do is contact each creditor to work out a new payment plan. You will be surprised at how willing a lender can be to work out a payment plan with you. So many times, we will not even answer the phone to talk with them so we do not put ourselves in a position to receive help. We let our emotions get the best of us. We feel ashamed, angry, sad, or disappointed with ourselves about the situation and decide that there is nothing we can do about it, but more times than not there is always something that can be done. We just have to contact the lender and talk with someone about our options.

The purpose of working out a new payment plan is to pay down that debt and establish a new history of paying on time. The lender will gladly work something out with you especially if you have not been paying them in the past. They want their money too. They would rather work something out with you instead of not receiving anything at all.

If you are able to at least make the minimum payment, then that is sufficient but if that is not possible then send in something. Some form of payment is better than nothing. It will show the lender that you are making an effort to pay the debt. You may still be charged a late fee but it will keep the account from moving to the next level of collections, which really affects your credit. I have been in courtrooms and heard the judge tell a creditor that if the client is sending you something then you need to work with them because they are at least making an effort.

That takes us to the next item on the report that we should look at which is public records. Public records are the items that have been filed against you at the local city or county records department. Someone went in front of a judge to petition payment from you on a particular debt. This can result in judgments or liens against you. When you file for bankruptcy, you create a public record for yourself.

These are the result of those summonses we sometime receive in the mail or the sheriff's department delivers it to our door. We normally disregard them when we see on the form that we do not have to appear in court. The problem with that is we should always go to court in order to make an attempt at some payment arrangements with the creditor. Having judgments and liens on your report are devastating to your credit. Once they go on your report they cannot be removed until they are satisfied but if you've made some arrangements with the creditor then the account remains in collections, which has a less damaging effect on your overall credit than a judgment does.

I know that sitting in court listening to other people's dilemmas can be boring and sometimes intimidating but this is the price we have to pay for the decisions we have made. I know that every time I have gone to court just to appear for a warrant in debt or civil suit of some kind, I have always left with some payment arrangement that I made with the lawyer and knowing that I was in better shape than if I had not shown up. It took me a while to realize that if you just show up and face the music it usually is not as bad as we thought it would be.

Now the other item I mentioned pertaining to public records was bankruptcies. If you filed a Chapter 7 bankruptcy, which is the type that erases all of your debts, then you will have to wait at least two to four years from the discharge date to obtain a mortgage. If you filed a Chapter 13, which is a payment plan to your creditors, then you will have to wait until your plan is complete and the bankruptcy is discharged. Then you will have to wait at least another year to obtain a mortgage. The type of mortgage you apply for and the reason for your bankruptcy will be the deciding factors on the length of time you will need to wait.

I have different feelings about filing or not filing bankruptcy. Everyone's situation is different and should be looked at individually. I know I probably should have filed bankruptcy years ago but for different reasons as I explained earlier in the book I did not. If I had another chance, I probably would have filed a Chapter 7 just to give me a fresh start but hindsight is 20/20. I probably would have messed up my credit again after filing the bankruptcy anyway. You have to be mature enough to deal with certain situations in life or else you will just mess it up. I do believe that is why I was not able to file the bankruptcies on those different occasions. I was just not ready to handle the responsibility. If I would have cleared my credit and built it up again, I probably would have continued making bad decisions and placed myself in worse shape than before.

It's important to realize when you file bankruptcy, everyone will all of a sudden start to offer you credit. Those companies that denied you six months earlier will be begging to give you a credit card, car, furniture, etc… This is because they know if you do not pay, they can take you to court, garnish your wages, or place a lien on your belongings. You will no longer have the option of filing bankruptcy and starting over.

This credit thing takes discipline and maturity. You have to decide that you are not going to make those same stupid decisions that you made in the past. You have to decide that you are not going backwards anymore. That was my decision. I was just sick and tired of being sick and tired. It is one thing when you can blame someone for your situation but when you know that you are the real reason you are in the position you are in; it is a sickening feeling. You can only be mad at yourself.

I know thinking of the work you may have to do to fix your credit may seem insurmountable but I can tell you for a fact it is not. There was a time I owed over a hundred thousand dollars in debt and that did not include my mortgage. I would sit there, think about how much I owed, and think that I would never be able to pay that off. It would astound me at times. The thing I did was take it one-step at a time. I know that sounds like a cliché saying but it is the truth.

I started with the small bills first. That was hard only because the creditors for the large bills were really on me for payment. They were the ones taking me to court and garnishing my check. The large bills were placing liens on everything I owned or at least they thought I owned. I still just focused on the small bills first because when I paid off a couple of those bills it gave me a feeling of accomplishment. I knew I still owed a lot of money but paying off somebody allowed me to start feeling better about myself.

It took me awhile but I eventually got to the point where I paid off everyone. Some people had to agree to a reduced amount and some creditors actually wrote the debts off before I was able to pay them but the debts were forgiven. Now that I had finally paid off everyone, I had to start rebuilding my credit. I did not have any bills at that time and that felt good, but that did not help my credit situation.

Most people think if they do not owe anyone then they have good credit but that is not true. If you do not owe anyone then that is a good thing but if you do not have any open credit accounts then there is nothing the credit bureaus can look at to determine your current credit status. They are not concerned with what happened in the past, creditors want to know what your current status is. Therefore, it is always a good practice not to pay off all of your accounts. You should keep several accounts open and current. If you use them then pay them in full when the bill comes.

The thing that I started to do was primarily focus on paying my utilities on time. That was more than a notion. I was used to not paying them until I had received a termination notice. That was the first true discipline I had to develop. Many people are not aware that some of their utilities report to credit each month until they go to purchase something and find out that waiting until the last minute to pay the gas bill has hurt them. In some states, utilities do not report to credit, but lenders will allow you to provide proof of on time payments. This is called non-traditional credit. That really came in handy when it was time to purchase my home.

Secondly, I applied for a couple of secured credit cards. A secured credit card is a credit card that you must make a deposit towards before being allowed to use the card. The deposit is there if for some reason you do not make the payments, they can take it out of the deposit. Secured cards are good to use to re-establish credit because they will report your payment history to the credit bureaus.

I also went to the credit union where I banked and opened a secured signature loan. This loan works similar to the secured credit card in which you deposit the exact amount in which they are lending you. The deposit is there as collateral for the lender just in case you default on the loan. Once you have paid back the full amount then the deposit is used as a line of credit. This helps your credit rating because the credit union reports your payments to the credit bureaus.

The next thing I did was finance a car. Now this is not always the best way to improve your credit because when you finance a car, and your credit rating is not the best, you will end up with a ridiculous interest rate. Now if you have had credit problems in the past, I am sure you have never negotiated the interest rate or payment when you financed a car. You usually are only concerned with if you can afford the payment. You probably never even asked what the interest rate was or how much you will end up paying for the car if you pay it off through their finance plan. However, I needed a car and did not have any money to go and purchase one outright. I decided that I would make my payments on time for at least the first year then contact the creditor and negotiate a lower interest rate. That actually worked for me because they were able to see a positive payment history over a year period and were glad to reduce my interest rate, which also reduced my payment.

Now let me explain something. These things did not happen overnight. I did not open these accounts all at the same time. Each transaction required me to have some money at the beginning so I had to do them one at a time. It took me about a two-year period to open these accounts and establish my payment history with the utility companies. The entire time I was focused on the main objective though, which was buying my house.

Banking

I just mentioned that one of the ways I used to re-establish my credit was opening a secured loan with my credit union. Well in order to do that I had to have an account with a credit union. I want to take this section and discuss banking options. Most people in our community do not use traditional banks and credit unions. They either do not trust putting their money in these institutions or have had an account in the past and for one reason or another had the account closed with a negative balance, which means they are now listed in the national checking database as owing a bank some money. They may also be afraid to open an account fearing that some creditor may find out about it and place a lien on their account to pay for something else they are indebted for.

"Governments and public interest groups are concerned about people who do not have bank accounts. This group is less likely than people who have bank accounts to own a home, to get a loan, and so forth," explains the researcher, Ebonya Washington, Ph.D., of Yale University's Departments of Economics and Political Science and a faculty research fellow with the National Bureau of Economics. "Some have hypothesized that if you don't have access to mainstream financial centers; it makes it harder to secure the American dream and to be financially sound."

Some people rely on check cashing stores to cash their payroll, government, or personal checks. These corner stores charge customers very high fees for their check cashing needs. If you use check-cashing stores, you should be aware that there are less expensive ways to cash that check.

You can avoid paying high fees by opening or using a basic checking or savings account at a bank, savings and loan, or credit union. Think about the costs before using a check-cashing store.

The monthly fees for a basic checking account are usually less than the fee a check cashing store charges to cash just one check. Even if you do not have an account, most banks, savings and loans, and credit unions will cash government and payroll checks for less than the check cashing store charges. If you have previously had issues with a bank, do not get discouraged. Many banks now offer what they call "Second Chance" accounts.

I can relate to all of the previous concerns. I grew up hearing my father say that he did not trust the banks. He always cashed his paycheck at the local convenience store. The owner would charge him a few dollars to cash his check. The owner would also allow my father to "run up a tab" before he actually was paid. That gave my father the opportunity to buy food whenever we got low at home. The owner of the store would just take the amount of the tab out of my father's paycheck when he came in to cash it. This is the way my father cashed his paycheck for many years.

The only reason my father eventually opened a checking account at a bank was when he was retired and receiving a disability check. The Social Security Administration sent out a letter stating that in order for a person to receive their monthly benefits they would have to have a bank account to receive it through direct deposit. My father was over 60 years old by that time. Up until then he had been cashing his paycheck at the local convenience store.

Many of you can relate to my father's situation. You have either cashed your checks at the grocery store, pawnshop, loan shark, bootlegger house, or whatever. This is a consistent habit in our communities. The problem with this habit is mainly one thing. You have no record of your banking history when you work that way. There are many other disadvantages to not having a bank account but for the sake of purchasing a home, the main problem is you have no record of your banking history. The lender wants to see how you handle your money. They want to know if you spend all of your paycheck as soon as you get it and if you do, what are you spending it on? Are you paying your bills on time or are you shopping frivolously with the money?

Banking with a reputable bank or credit union has many advantages. You position yourself to receive certain benefits when you bank with most financial institutions. I know the credit unions I have dealt with in the past are more likely to approve a loan for you when you are a member. If you have been a member with them for a while and have never had any negative dealings there, you have a great chance of obtaining financing for a loan.

Most credit unions are member-managed, meaning the members of the credit union hold positions on the board of directors. They insure that the members of the credit union are treated fairly. Many credit unions will allow you to open an account with them even if you have had a negative experience at another institution. You just have to do some research and find out what the requirements are to open an account.

One of the things I did and suggest for everyone to do is open a savings account for your children. Teach them how to deal with a bank by allowing them to accompany you to the bank. Show them how to deposit money in and withdraw money out. So many children think that all mommy or daddy have to do is go to the money machine and take money out or just write a check for it. They do not realize that you have to put some money in the bank before you can take any out.

We have to teach our children to handle and respect money. We have to break the generational curse that runs in our families. You may not realize it but your children will pick up your financial habits just like any other habit. The same way a child who was raised in a house in which their parents smoked is likely to smoke themselves. That same child will also pick up the financial habits of their parents.

I can attest to that myself. I picked up all of my father's bad habits. My father was an alcoholic and I was on my way to being one. Thank God, I stopped drinking over 20 years ago. My father had horrible money habits and died broke. I had those same money habits and it took me until I was forty years old to overcome them. I have noticed that my eldest child has developed those same financial habits of spending every dime she makes. I am attempting to teach her by example to break those habits so that she will not have to wait until she is forty to overcome them.

Now there are some other banking options just in case you are not able to open an account at this time. Several companies allow you to open a checking account through a debit card. The way it works is you deposit your money with the particular institution and they issue you a debit card with either a MasterCard or a Visa logo on it. You can withdraw cash from the ATM with these cards. You can use the card to purchase items just like a regular credit card. You can also set up to have your paycheck direct deposited and use the card to pay bills.

The only difference is you must have the cash in the account in order to use the card. This is actually a good thing because this way you cannot accumulate a balance like you would with a credit card. The only downfall to these type cards is some of them have high fees associated with using the cards. There are some companies whose fees are not outrageous. I used Walmart's debit card for a couple of years during a period that I was not able to open a checking account at the bank. You just need to do some research and find out what are the fees.

<u>Budget</u>

The first step to setting a proper example for your children is to establish a household budget. I know for me, the thought of a budget never crossed my mind. I had been treading water for so long just trying to keep my head above the water, the thought of actually swimming to shore never happened. I used to think that a budget was only for those people who had more than enough money. It was to make sure that you did not spend more than you really wanted to spend. I thought it was not for those of us who did not have enough money. We were too busy trying to find a way to create more money instead of managing the money that we did have.

A budget takes discipline, which is something that is not common for most of us. Not everyone has the discipline to stick to a budget but everyone has the ability to learn the discipline necessary for a budget. The way I was able to establish a budget was to look at my family household as a business. The Family Business so to speak. I have had several businesses over the years. Some of them were successful and some failed from day one. The thing that was constant with the successful businesses was that we had an operating budget.

An operating budget is an itemized list of everything that is needed to operate the business. We made sure that those items were taken care of as a priority. We knew that if they were not then we were probably not going to make any money. We also did not spend any money that was not in the budget mainly because the money was not in abundance and we could not afford to spend it.

Before opening the business, my partners and I would sit down and create a business plan with an operating budget. The business plan contained the objectives for the business. It detailed why we were in business, what we plan to accomplish while in business, and how we planned to do it. The operating budget was listed in the "how to" section. It detailed our projected revenue and expenses. We would go over the budget as a team and eliminate anything that was not necessary. The main thing we always did was come to an agreement that if it was not in the budget then it was not necessary at that time.

That is exactly the same way I set up my budget at home. I sat down with my wife and listed every bill we had. We first determined which bills was priority meaning they had to be paid no matter what happen. They were listed in the order of importance:

1. Rent
2. Lights
3. Water
4. Food
5. Car
6. Credit Cards
7. Phone
8. Furniture
9. Internet
10. Cable

These bills had to be paid every month. We listed our incomes down and determined which bills would be paid on what part of the month. For instance, the rent had to be paid by the fifth of every month. The other bills had different due dates but were usually during the same part of each month. It may help to take your must pay list and separate it into multiple lists based on due date and how often you are paid.

We then listed the things that we spent money on but were not a necessity. Such as:

- Pizza every Friday and Chinese every other Friday
- Going to the movies
- Clothes shopping
- Beauty salon and barbershop
- Nail salon
- Going out to dinner
- Buying CD's and DVD's
- Going out for lunch

These were the items that we decided had to either be eliminated all together or at least reduced. These were actually the hardest part of the budget to control. We had developed habits of doing these things for so long that it was difficult to stop. That is where the discipline came into play. We had to help each other stick to the budget especially when the kids were attempting to manipulate one of us.

We had to involve our children in the plan. They had to have an understanding of why we suddenly could not order pizza on Friday anymore. They needed to know that we were not going to the mall on the weekends or going out to dinner after church on Sundays. They needed to realize that their mother would be doing their hair for the most part and they would not be going to the beauty shop every other week. It was important to explain to them why they could not have money every weekend to go to the movies. Therefore, we sat down as a family and told them the plan.

I told them that we as a family had to change our spending habits. We were spending money on things that did not really matter and we could not afford to continue to do that. I told them that the family was going to stick to a budget. I then explained to them what a budget was and why it was important to stick to it. This gave them an understanding of why we would not be doing the things they were used to doing because as crazy as it sounds, even during the really tough times, we were still spending money on stupid stuff. There was times when the lights were off and I gave my kids money to go to the mall. I mainly did it to get them out of the house so that I would not have to feel ashamed in front of them, but that was still very stupid. I needed to save every penny I had to get the lights back on instead of giving money to my children to go to the mall.

I also explained to them what the goal was at the time. I feel you should always have a goal for your family and your kids should know about it. I told them that we were focusing on buying a new home. I even had some brochures of different homes I had been looking at. Children are visual creatures and I knew that would help them understand. I even took a couple of the pictures and taped them to the refrigerator so that everyone could always keep the goal in mind. This allowed my kids to understand why we were doing what we were doing and it made it easier on my wife and me because when the kids understood why we were cutting back on stuff they stopped begging for everything.

Now back to the budget. After listing everything we could cut out we also listed the costs of all of the things on that list to get an idea of how much money we were spending on unnecessary things. The amount really startled me. Let me give you an example:

- Pizza every Friday $125/month
- Going to the movies $80/month
- Clothes shopping $225/month
- Beauty salon and barbershop $425/month
- Going out to dinner every other Sunday $225/month
- Eating out during the week $250/month
- Buying CD's and DVD's $100/month
- Going out for lunch $175/month

TOTAL per month: **$1,605**

I could not believe the amount of money we were spending on stuff that was not necessary every month. That was almost $20,000 a year. That was ridiculous. It still upsets my stomach when I think about it. I am sure if you sat down and did the same thing, it would blow your mind as well.

Once my wife and I realized how much money we were blowing each month, we were determined to change. Now I wish I could tell you that it was all peaches and cream from that point but I would be telling a big lie. We absolutely struggled with the budget. In the beginning, we were all gung ho about it but that only lasted about two months. Life just wore us down in the beginning. The kids lost their focus after about two weeks and the begging began. I tried to be hard at first but they wore me down. Therefore, the budget plan became a roller coaster ride.

We would stick to it for a month and then not do it for a couple of months. Then we would have a motivational meeting and start it up again. This went on for a couple of years before we actually disciplined ourselves to stick with the plan. I know that is not what you really wanted to hear but I told you that I was going to shoot straight with you. Sticking to a budget is not an easy thing and I do not want you to think that it is but it is a necessary thing. I knew that without a budget my family business was failing.

It was just like the businesses I had before. The ones that ran on a budget normally succeeded. The ones in which we got away from the budget usually did not prosper. I had to start running my family like a business. When I gave my children an "allowance," I actually wrote them a check. I then took them to the bank and opened up a savings account for them. They had to deposit the check into their account in order to get their money.

I taught them to take 10% of the money to pay their tithes at church. I also taught them to leave at least 10% in the bank for savings. I found out from the guy who does my taxes that since I was "paying" them their allowances by check, I could write off a percentage of that on my taxes just like if they were employees of my business. I think the actual amount that could be deducted was $2,500.00 per child. Check with your tax preparer to be sure but that is a significant amount of money that can be used as a tax deduction.

I know you are saying this sounds like "The Brady Bunch" or "The Cosby Show" or something and trust me it could not be farther from that. It took me a LONG TIME to get to this point. I mean a LOOOONG TIME.

I knew that the main component to getting my finances in order was the budget. Once I finally disciplined myself to stick to it, I saw the benefits instantly. The budget was the only reason we were able to save any money. It was the main reason we were able to pay off the debts we owed and get our credit in good standing.

The budget is the most important part for anyone to stabilize their financial status. It does not matter how much money you bring in, if there is not a budget in place that can help you control your spending then you are destined to fail. For years, I felt that I just needed to make more money and everything would be all right but that was not true. The more money I made the more I spent and I was still always BROKE. The budget changed my life.

Sticking to a budget requires discipline and persistency. I read the book, "Think and Grow Rich: A Black Choice" by Napoleon Hill and Dr Dennis Kimbro. In that book, they wrote this about Earl Graves, the founder of Black Enterprise magazine:

> "In high school in Brooklyn's Bedford-Stuyvesant section, Graves sold his relentless energy by working three jobs at once. At Morgan State, he paid his way through college by working as a swim instructor and dorm counselor. He even ran track for his meal ticket.
>
> Graves majored in economics, and by his junior year launched a landscaping business from his dorm room. He had a friend type a flyer that promised

experienced lawn service at reasonable rates, and he stuffed every mailbox in sight. Anticipating only a modest response, he was totally unprepared for what followed. *More than forty homeowners signed up the first week!*

Graves graduated from college and entered the Army in 1958. Here, he developed and sharpened his sales skills. Though he made first lieutenant ahead of schedule, the military was clearly not a career; Graves had other things on his mind. When he completed his tour, he went back to New York and tried his hand in real estate.

In his first three months, he sold nine houses-enough to pay for a wedding and furnish a modest apartment. In 1965, Graves went to work for the Justice Department, a job that would eventually lead to his working for Robert Kennedy, then a New York senator. Working for Kennedy introduced Graves to a world he had never seen: a world where power was a natural heritage; where the word cannot did not exist, and where everybody practiced salesmanship.

'Working for the senator played an enormous part in my personal development,' said Graves. 'Robert Kennedy was a man who was totally unfamiliar with failure.'

Graves recalled an incident where he was asked by the senator to contact then Secretary of the Interior Morris Udall. At the time, Udall was vacationing in Colorado, rafting down one of its more popular rivers. After several unsuccessful attempts to contact the secretary, Graves informed Kennedy that he was unable to reach Udall. To this the senator crisply responded, 'Graves, that raft is not going down that river all day. It's going to stop somewhere, *and when it does, I want Udall standing there with a phone in his hand!' Those words still penetrate Graves' psyche today.*

That story is a part of my personal philosophy. You would be surprised how many people quit when faced with obstacles. As every good salesman knows, everything may not be possible today-but sooner or later, it is possible.

For nearly twenty years, Earl Graves would apply this maxim as he and a cadre of loyal employees strove to keep Black Enterprise magazine at the forefront of the business-monthly circulation charts."

I decided to tell that story to let you know that no matter the obstacle that is in front of you, you can still overcome it. It has been proven time and time again.

I can personally attest to this. For a long while, it seemed as though I would never get out of that canyon of debt and regain some sense of integrity. I think that bothered me more than anything else did. The feeling that people were looking at me as a "dead beat"; someone who never pays anybody and owes everybody. I felt as though everywhere I went I was going to bump into someone that I owed money. That feeling drove me half-crazy. However, through discipline, determination, and persistency I was able to rise above the problems I created.

Therefore, now that we have worked on our credit, established a banking relationship of some sort, and setup a budget to stabilize our finances; it is now time to ***get in the game***.

Part Three

Game Time

"What we, the colored people want, is character. And this nobody can give us. It is something we must earn for ourselves."

Frederick Douglas

Now that we have discussed our adventures of destroying our credit and our financing. We also have discussed how to repair our situation and prepare ourselves for the next move. Now, it is time for us to make that first major step into the world of homeownership. I emphasize the word first, because we will discuss later on in this book how to use this step as a stepping-stone to bigger and better things, but let's not get ahead of ourselves.

In this section, we will go over the loan approval process. We will discuss how to select a real estate agent. We will detail selecting that dream home and the reason I say "dream home" is because for the majority of us buying a home was only a dream in our minds but not anymore. We will go over the entire loan process from application to picking up your keys at closing. Lastly, we will discuss what you should expect after closing on the house once you are living in it.

However, before we move into this section we must first work on our own way of thinking. We must change that inner conversation that is going on within our heads. It is that voice that continues to tell you, *"You know you cannot get that house."* It says, *"You know you are only dreaming and dreaming is for fools."* It continues, *"Nobody else in the family has a house so why do you think you can get one? You are no better than anyone else is. If they could not get one you know you won't be able to."*

You must change that inner conversation from negative and degrading to positive and uplifting. You have to tell yourself that you are worthy of buying a house. You can change your financial situation. You can manage your money better. Tell yourself that you deserve the best that life has to offer. Tell yourself that you deserve to find your purpose in life. You have to do this because there is probably no one else to tell you these things.

It is crucial for you to believe these things about yourself. This process is not going to be easy. I would be lying to you if I told you it was. If it were easy, everyone would have done it. That is why you have to decide in your mind and heart that no matter what happens you are going to make it to your goal. That first goal is buying your home. This will position you for bigger and better things down the road.

So determine in your heart that you are ready to attack life because that is the only way to live. Henry David Thoreau suggested that most people of his times led lives of "quiet desperation" and not much has changed. He offered the thought, *"Oh to reach the point of death only to realize that I have never really lived."* Determine in your mind that you are going to attack life and live your dreams. I heard Les Brown say once, *"There is no safe position in life. You must attack it. You cannot get out of life alive. So get on the field and into the game."*

Loan Approval

I always tell people do not go with the first bank, credit union, or mortgage broker you meet. I know you may feel that you are lucky if anyone is willing to work with you but believe me once you get yourself in position to qualify for a loan then there are a lot of people who will be willing to help you. So do not just go with the first person who says that they can get you done. I suggest that you ask around. Find someone who has already gone through the process and ask them these questions:

- Who was your lender?
- How long has the loan officer been in the mortgage business?
- Did you like your loan officer?
- Was he/she efficient? Did they work in a timely manner?
- Were they considerate of your wants and needs?
- Did they allow you to see your credit report?
- Did they offer you various programs to choose from?
- Did they answer the phone when you called or were they
  quick in returning your call?
- Did they seem to know what they were doing?
- How long did it take you to close from start to finish?
- Did they follow-up with you after the closing?

These questions are very important. Do not be ashamed or embarrassed to ask them either. This is an "interview process" and you are the interviewer. Remember unless that loan officer is planning to make those mortgage payments for you every month you are in charge. They work for you. People always feel that just because their credit is not perfect they have to go into the bank or lender's office with their "hat in their hands" begging for a loan.

First of all, the loan officer is receiving some kind of commission from this loan so they want to close it just as bad as you do. If a loan officer ever makes you feel inferior, you should thank them for their time, get up, and walk out. There is one thing that I have found out over the last decade of being in this business. If one loan officer can get a deal done then so can another one. There is no deal that only one person is capable of closing. Now let me add something to that as well, do not go in there thinking you can ask for the world. You will probably be limited to two maybe three programs depending on your credit scores so do not get crazy with the notion of being in charge.

The reason it is important to like the loan officer is that you will be working with this person for probably 30-45 days. I have seen many instances where the clients could not stand the loan officer. I have seen clients get into arguments with the loan officers but continue to work with them because they were scared to move on to someone else. I feel it is important to have some kind of positive working relationship with the loan officer. You do not have to fall in love with them but at least get along.

You need to know how long they have been in the financial services business. I say financial services because they could have been in another section of the business such as banking, insurance, or stock market. Either of those divisions will let you know that they are familiar with the industry. You want to know if they are experienced or not because an experienced loan officer can foresee certain problems and will know how to overcome those obstacles without panicking. Someone who has been in the business a while has probably experienced many different situations. I always tell my clients that a loan process without any bumps or obstacles is the exception. Most loans always have some issue to deal with. You just find out what is needed and give the underwriter what they are asking for.

It is important to find out if they are normally efficient with their work. You do not want to have someone who keeps losing your information. You filled out an application with them on one occasion and when you call to check the status, they cannot even find your file. Therefore, you have to go there again and fill out another application. That is very frustrating and not a confidence gainer for you toward your loan officer. You also do not want someone who tells you one time frame and keep changing it as you go along. They start saying the loan process will take three weeks and then three months later you still are not even close to closing your loan.

You want someone who is considerate to your needs. They should answer the phone when you call or at least return the call in a timely manner. Now do not get me wrong, I have had some clients who thought that I should only work with them. They felt that they were the only ones who mattered and I should always put their needs before others. I try to make all of my clients feel special but I also let them know that there are other clients that I have to show the same amount of attention to as well. Most people just want you to be honest with them and help them as quickly as possible.

The loan officer should be very thorough when filling out the application because any little detail can change the loan process completely. For instance, let's say while completing the application the loan officer asks you how much do you make on your job. He fills in the amount and then moves on to the next section. After completing the application, he later calculates your debt to income ratio and determines that you do not make enough money. He calls you at home and leaves a message stating that you did not qualify for the loan.

Now he does not know that you have a part-time job that you have been at for over two years as well as receiving a child support check through the state from your child's father. You did not know to tell him because he did not ask about any other income. Therefore, he made a decision without having all of the necessary information. It happens all of the time. An experienced loan officer will know to be thorough. They will know that this could make or break a loan.

You want a loan officer that will involve you in the process. What I mean by that is he goes over your credit report with you. He does not just browse over it without asking you about each item on the report. I always give my clients a copy of their report and then we go over it line by line. I feel everyone needs to see what is being reported about him or her. There can be a lot of erroneous information on the credit report that can cause people not to qualify for a loan.

After going over the report with you, the loan officer should then discuss with you the programs you qualify for. He should give you several options and explain each one. There are several types of mortgages but the main two are fixed-rate and adjustable-rate mortgages (ARMs). A fixed-rate is a loan in which the interest rate stays the same throughout the duration of the loan. An adjustable-rate is a loan in which the rate is fixed for a determined period and then it adjusts periodically.

Let us address the scare about adjustable-rate mortgages. Currently in our country, we are experiencing what the federal government has termed a "mortgage and housing crisis." They feel this is due to sub-prime lending in which many people received adjustable-rate mortgages and now they are adjusting and people cannot afford the payment. In the beginning, they were really coming down on the loan officers for placing individuals in these loans.

In the U.S., people always feel a need to pass blame on someone or some group for any and everything that happens. Therefore, for the "mortgage crisis" they passed the blame on loan officers. The media stated that "predatory lenders" convinced individuals to use adjustable-rate mortgages and if they had not then those individuals would not have been in the position of losing their homes. Now I have said all along that for the most part loan officers only used this program to offer clients a way of purchasing more home for their clients. In addition, the loan officers do not create the programs; they only sell the programs. Lastly, the individuals need to take responsibility for the mortgages that they purchased. It's important that you read and understand everything that you sign. At the end of the day, you are agreeing to the terms and are responsible for the payment. If you don't understand something, ask!

I know that the entire mortgage process is very intimidating and that there is a lot of paperwork involved with language that is hard to understand but that does not excuse adults for signing their names to loan applications and deeds agreeing to terms that may seem a little ridiculous. I know over the past ten years of closing loans whether it was a purchase or refinance, I have had maybe five people who actually read the papers they were signing. Every closing that I have ever attended I tell the people to make sure they understand what they are signing. They always look at me and say, *"I trust you Dave."* In which I reply, *"I don't want you to trust me. Please read the papers and ask questions about them."*

People never want to take the time to read what it is they are signing. A mortgage is the largest financial obligation that an individual will obtain in their life. Why wouldn't you take the time to read the papers? That is why every closing must have an attorney oversee the paperwork just in case there are legal questions or if the paperwork is not completed according to the agreed upon conditions. People come to the closing excited either about purchasing a new home or about refinancing their mortgage in which they will probably receive a settlement check. They are anxious to complete the transaction and move on. I have been saying it for over a decade; please have an understanding of what you are committing yourself to.

I can say with a little pride that I have never had a client whose mortgage payment adjusted without them having full expectation of it. Whenever I placed an individual in an ARM, we did it with a plan of action, meaning we decided what was going to happen with that mortgage. We either agreed upon a date to either refinance the mortgage or on several occasions sell the property before the adjustment period began. That was the whole purpose of that type of loan. It allowed an individual to begin their mortgage with a lesser payment allowing them to slowly adjust to the mortgage. Most people used the mortgage when they knew their income was about to increase in a few years. I also had several clients who knew that they would only be in that house for a short period due to job or family obligations and thus had a lower payment than with a fixed-rate mortgage. This was also the ideal mortgage for investors who only wanted the smallest payment.

The problem with many loan officers is they do not establish a relationship with their clients. Especially during the "refinance boom" when any and everyone was able to obtain a mortgage, and there were more loan officers in the business than ever before. In many states, they did not have to have any license or training. They just needed to know how to fill out an application. The problem was they probably knew as much if not less than the clients themselves but were able to close loans and make a good income. Therefore, they essentially became "paper pushers," not establishing a relationship with the client only filling out an application and pushing it to the next department.

I admit that is exactly what I was doing in the beginning of my loan officer career. The problem I had was that most of the people I was dealing with had credit issues so I had to work with them awhile before I was able to qualify them for a loan. While working with them I learned how important that relationship was. It made the process a lot easier and it gave me my bread and butter: referrals.

So let us get back to our interview of the loan officer. You should ask them what the entire loan process entails. They should be able to give you systematic expectations of the process. They should have some type of communication system in place whether it is by email, phone, or a website. Nowadays, it is easier to communicate with an individual through email. Most people access their emails daily and a lot of them multiple times throughout the day.

I like to use my website as well as email. I give my clients a username and password in which they can log in to my pipeline and see their loan. They can follow the process of their loan and see if there is anything that they need to complete. People like to be included in the process. It gives them a sense of security knowing what is going on. I found out that this way works a lot better than contacting them on the phone just to tell them where we are in the process.

If the loan officer does not have a website, it is okay. They just have not caught up to today's technology just yet. Do not hold that against them. It could be their company who is late getting in the game. Whatever their communication system is, they need to utilize it. If they only use the phone then they should have a policy of answering every call or at least returning every message within an hour. If they use the email system only then their policy should be to return every email by the end of the day. They need to have some policy in which they can be held accountable for.

The step-by-step process should go from the initial phone call to the follow-up after the closing. The process should explain how they plan to fill out the application, whether you need to come into the office or can they complete it over the phone. They should tell you every document that they need of you in the beginning. This is important to know upfront especially if it is something that you may have to order from somewhere.

For example, if they need you to provide the last twelve months bank statements. You probably do not have them accessible and will have to contact your financial institution. Most banks and credit unions will have to research this information and then send them to you so that takes time. If you need copies of your 401k and IRA statements, you will probably have to order them. If you know this in advance then you will have time to order them for the loan officer.

The systematic process should explain to you if there are any upfront fees expected from you such as credit report, house inspection, or appraisals. Some loan officers do not ask the client to pay for the credit reports but some require that you give them a credit card to pay for your credit report. This can run from $8 to $25 depending on the lender. I know most clients are expected to pay for their appraisals usually when the appraiser does the report. This can cost the client from $350-500 depending on the area and type of report requested. If a home inspection is required, this can cost the client from $100-250 depending on the type of report. These fees can quickly add up especially if you are not aware of them ahead of time.

The step-by-step process should inform you of how long you should expect to wait to get to closing. They should be able to give you a good estimate. Now there are things that can happen that are out of the loan officer's control. For example, if the underwriter orders a field review for the appraisal. They do this at times because the appraisers sometime get creative with their reports and may list comparable properties that do not really exist. Therefore, the lender will require an additional appraiser review the report, and verify that the facts included are accurate. This includes driving past the property and comparables. This can slow down a loan process.

The underwriting department of a lender can slow down a loan process and there is really nothing a loan officer can do about it but wait it out. The loan officer does not want to keep calling the underwriter harassing them about your loan. This could back fire on you. If you irritate an underwriter, they may decide to "nitpick" every little detail of the loan. It could be something that they would normally let go but since the loan officer has "ticked" them off, they may decide to ask for it.

It's also important to realize that underwriters have guidelines and rules they must follow, and depending on the experience of your loan officer in collecting documents at the beginning, may ask for additional items. Such as bank statements, usually an underwriter only wants 2-3 months bank statements so that they can see a pattern of deposits and withdrawals in the client's account. Current guidelines require that the underwriter question any large deposits that are not clearly payroll checks, which requires that the loan officer take the time after consulting with the client to write letters of explanation, provide supporting documentation and send it all in.

I always tell my clients that if they ask for something then just give it to them. If it is something we do not have then that is when I call to negotiate another option. An experienced loan officer knows to send in a complete loan package to avoid as many delays as possible.

I have dealt with some great underwriters and I have dealt with some Napoleon-type people. Most underwriters are strictly salary people so they will be paid whether they close your deal or not. Most loan officers are commission paid people so they are trying to do whatever they can to get that deal done. The problem with that is people have a tendency to move in the direction of the unethical and immoral when money comes into the picture. Loan officers have been known to do some underhanded things just to be paid.

That is why most underwriters are salary paid people; the lenders do not want to give a person with that much control an incentive to do the wrong thing. If they were strictly commission paid individuals then they would make sure that every deal that came across their desk was approved and closed which would mean that they would approve some deals that did not deserve to be approved. Therefore, it is a good thing that they are not driven to push every deal through but sometimes they can really frustrate a loan officer by going through every deal with a fine toothed comb.

If you run into a situation such as this, the loan officer should be able to explain to you what is going on and what to expect from the situation. Now I have to defend the loan officer, sometimes we actually do not know what is going on because it could just be sitting on someone's desk. It's important to understand that some lenders to not allow the loan officer access to the underwriter, and they truly have limited information during this part of the process. That is a very frustrating situation for a loan officer. They do not know what is going on and they have you calling them to find out. The client considers the loan officer as the lender. They really do not understand the entire process and really do not care to know. All they know is they met with someone who represented the lender and as far as they are concerned, that someone should be able to handle all situations.

Okay before we continue with the description of the closing process, let us finish our focus on the selection of the loan officer. I do not want to get ahead of myself. After the loan officer goes over the steps of the loan process, they should first qualify you for the loan. In order to qualify you, the loan officer will have to complete a loan application. They will ask you several questions from name, address, date of birth, social security number, employment income, and various other items. They will run a credit report on you to view your scores and listed obligations. They will determine first by your scores if you qualify for any loan programs that are available.

Now this is where things can become a little tricky. It will depend on what type of lender a loan officer works for that determines what types of loan programs that are available. If they work for a local bank then the number of programs will be limited. Most local banks only offer a small number of programs for loans and they are designed for individuals with very good credit. If the loan officer works for an independent mortgage broker who has access to various lenders then the amount of loan programs will be greater. That is because a broker has the ability to "shop" your loan to different lenders where a bank loan officer can only offer you the programs available at that particular bank. I receive referred loans from associates who work at banks with limited programs on a weekly basis.

I have been an independent mortgage broker my entire time in the business and I absolutely love the flexibility it allows me. I have a better chance of helping anyone who contacts me for a loan. I have access to lenders who only deal with clients with perfect credit and I have access to lenders who deal with clients with challenged credit. Now there are many stereotypes about mortgage brokers and I believe that real estate agents created them.

One of the main stereotypes is that brokers will charge you more than a bank. Now this is based on the individual broker. Some brokers charge a client for everything under the sun. They charge for the credit report, the application fee, an origination fee, a broker fee, a processing fee, and any other fee that they can get away with.

This again goes back to the individual broker and this is why you need to do your research. Now I am going to be honest with you. If you have many challenges on your credit and the loan officer has to do a lot of work to get your deal done then they are probably going to charge you a lot more than if you had perfect credit. I mean it is what it is. I know I charge more when I have to do more work and less when I have to do less work. I tell my clients upfront what to expect. That is fair to me because when the client's credit situation requires a lot of work to get the loan closed then they probably could not go to a local bank to get a loan.

Also, let me explain to you how a loan officer is paid. This will probably get me into some trouble with my fellow loan officers but I believe in letting people know what the deal is and how everything works. You see a loan officer is paid solely by either charging you, the client, an origination, discount, or broker fee. They call them points. A point is one percent of the loan amount. For example, if the loan amount is $100,000 then one point is $1,000.

In addition, the lender also can pay them by a yield spread percentage (ysp) which is referred to as being paid on the back end. The lender pays the loan officer based on the type of loan, whether it is a high-risk loan or not and the interest rate. The lender pays different amounts to the loan officer based on what interest rate they sell you on. So for instance, you may qualify for a base rate of 6.5%, which pays the loan officer nothing, but if they are able to sell you on a rate of 6.75% then the lender will pay them maybe .5% in ysp. Therefore, for a $100,000 loan that is a difference of $500 for the loan officer.

Now a lot of banks like to portray to you as if they are not making any money off the loan but the only reason they can get away with saying that is because they are not required to disclose to the client how much of a yield spread they are making on a loan. The brokers are the only ones who are required to show this amount thus making them seem to be greedy to the clients. Lastly, the loan officer can be paid by a combination of upfront fees, i.e. origination, broker, processing, discounts, and back-end fees, i.e. yield spread premiums.

Many brokers get nervous when going over the fees because they feel that the clients will try to negotiate a lower fee and they have the right to do that. When I first started originating loans, I used to feel the same way. That feeling was mainly because I did not feel confident in what I was doing and did not realize the value of it. It took me several years before I concluded that I am good at what I do. I am offering a service that has a lot of value and I deserve every dime that I charge for those services.

I have had some clients decide to go somewhere else because they felt my fees were too high but they were only shopping for a cheap loan anyway. I do not deal with shoppers. I do not deal with people calling me to ask what my rates are because since I am a broker my rates are the same as anyone else. As a broker, I have the ability to broker a loan with any lender that is available and receive the same rate as that bank if not a better rate. So when people call me to ask what my rates are I always ask them what rate are they looking for? If that rate is a reasonable one then I can give it to them if they qualify for it.

The next stereotype directed towards brokers is that brokers do not close loans. This is a huge misconception. Any account executive for a wholesale bank will tell you that the majority of their business comes from independent brokers. Closing a loan is based on submitting a qualified and complete loan package. The individual loan officer and their processor determine if they have one. If a loan officer does not submit a complete package then that will create delays. Also again a lot of these stereotypes if not all of them were created by real estate agents. Real estate agents and loan officers have a unique relationship. One feels that the other needs them more, so this creates a tense environment at times.

Personally, I am not crazy about many real estate agents because of the experiences I have had. I am not saying that this applies to all real estate agents but the ones I have dealt with are very arrogant and always try to tell me how to do my job. This is a problem for me because I do not need someone to tell me how to do my job when I have been doing it very well for quite awhile. Now do not get me wrong, I do have a few real estate agents who are my friends but not many. My feelings have always been that I can close a loan and make money without a real estate agent but they always need a loan officer to close a deal and be paid. So who really needs whom? That is all I am going to say about that.

     Okay back to the qualification process. The loan officer will determine which program you qualify for and at what rate. They should go over your projected mortgage payment with principal and interest and then including taxes and insurance. You may have an option to pay your taxes and insurance with your payment or pay them separately on your own. There are several factors that go into determining if you have the choice, including the type of loan you are applying for. The loan officer should then give you a loan approval letter for you to give to the real estate agent that you decide to use. The letter will detail to the agent exactly the amount you have qualified for, the interest rate, type of loan, and needed items for closing such as contract, appraisal, etc.

     Here is an example of an approval letter:

July 16, 2008

Client: Jane Doe

Property: 5555 ABC Blvd, Patriotic City, VA 12345

The Mortgage Therapist is pleased to confirm the above referenced individual(s) has made an application for a mortgage loan. She has been conditionally approved for a purchase price of $400,000 with a loan at 90% LTV in the amount not to exceed $360,000 for a term of 360 months at a rate not to exceed 7.5 % based on information presented by the borrower(s).

A mortgage credit report has been reviewed and it appears that the information provided meets underwriting criteria for a conventional loan. The following information must be presented and deemed acceptable by a qualified underwriter before a final approval can be granted.

1. A ratified purchase agreement
2. An appraisal of the property supporting the estimated value
3. A clean title history of the property

This approval is contingent upon the previous listed conditions. This approval is valid until August 31, 2014.

Sincerely,

Davian Clifton

This leads us to our next section, which is interviewing the real estate agent. This is a crucial part of your home buying process. The right real estate agent can make this experience a joyous occasion or a nightmare from hell. This interview is just as important as the interview for the loan officer. I always suggest to my clients to only deal with a real estate agent from a referral. I feel that you need to know that this individual will be the right one for you. That can only come from someone's personal experience with a particular agent.

You need to address certain questions:

- How experienced is the agent?
- How successful are they?
- Did they find you the type of house you were looking for?
- Are they working with a reputable firm?
- Did you like the agent as a person?
- Did the agent contact the client on a regular basis?
- Was the agent knowledgeable about the homes they were showing?
- Did they focus on homes that you can afford?
- How much did they charge you?
- How long did it take to find that home?

These are important questions to assist you in the selection process. I say selection process because just like the loan officer the real estate agent is working for you. You need to realize that in order to stay in charge of the situation but again do not get carried away with the feeling of being in charge and start demanding ridiculous things. You have already sat down with the loan officer and determined what you can afford. Now whether that amount is in the range you were looking for does not matter. What you can afford is what you can afford. It is as simple as that.

Do not allow a real estate agent or anyone else attempt to talk you into more house than you can afford. Remember what you qualify for and what is comfortable for you to pay are two different things. You may qualify for a $400,000 loan based on your income and credit but are only comfortable paying a loan of $285,000 based on your other obligations and goals. This is what the experts feel created the mortgage crisis from 2005 to 2009. People purchased more home than they truly could afford. They decided that they wanted the $400,000 home instead of that $285,000. Now realize this, real estate agents just like loan officers are paid commission on a closed deal. Their commission is based on the purchase price you pay. So of course, they would like you to purchase that $400,000 home instead of that $285,000 home.

For a loan officer, who on a good deal may make 3% of the loan amount, a real estate agent normally makes 6% of the purchase price. Let's say you are looking to purchase a house with 10% down. On the $400,000 house, your loan officer would make 3% of the $360,000 loan amount, or $10,800 in commission. The real estate agent would make $21,600. On the $285,000 house, your loan officer would make $7,695 while the real estate agent makes $15,390.

That is why a real estate agent and the loan officer may push you toward the higher amount. Now you are probably saying that they are wrong for doing that but let us be real. They are both salesmen who both work on commission. So if they are able to talk you into a higher amount when you know you are not comfortable with that amount then you are the fool not them. They are just working trying to make a dollar and you cannot hold that against them.

This can really turn into a sticky situation because a home for $285,000 is a lot different from a home at $400,000. It is like looking to buy a nice Toyota but really wanting a Lexus. You know you can handle the payments for the Toyota but that Lexus looks so good. You should not even get in that Lexus because once you drive it you cannot get back in the Toyota and convince yourself that they are the same. Therefore, the best thing is to stay in your range and a good real estate agent can help you do this.

Next, you really need to know if you can get along with the agent. It may take you several months to find the house that you are looking for so you really need to know if you can deal with going to different homes and probably riding with this agent. You need to know if they are going to really work for you or if they just sit back hoping that you find the house yourself and they are paid for it. A good agent is a hustler. They are always looking and working for their clients.

You need to know how successful this agent is. How many homes have they sold over the past few years? Their success can tell you if they are aggressive and organized. It is very hard to be successful without being aggressive and organized. Their success will let you know if they really know what they are doing or not. It will also let you know if they are in a position financially where they will not make decisions based on money.

Let me explain what I mean more clearly. Let's say you have an agent who has not closed a loan in several months. That agent is in desperate need of some money. Whenever a person is in need of money, they are in position to make bad decisions. Decisions based on money are not always the best decisions. A successful agent has been closing deals and is probably not in a position to make decisions based solely on money. Now I am not saying that someone who is new to the business cannot work out as well but that is something you will have to make a judgment call on for yourself.

The agent needs to be someone with a personality you can deal with. For instance if they are over the top excited all the time and you are a laid-back person, they may get on your nerves after a while. Now maybe their extrovert personality is the reason they are successful in the real estate business so you may want to deal with their perkiness to find the house you are looking for.

The agent should also have a complete understanding of the type of house you are looking for. You do not want to waste your time riding around looking at houses that are not the type of house you want to live in. For instance, you have a family of five and your mother is going to live with you as well. She had back surgery two years ago and cannot climb a set of stairs on a daily basis so you really need a four-bedroom ranch house. It does you no good if your agent keeps taking you to two story townhomes or third floor condominiums. They probably are nice houses but it is not what you are looking for.

Just like the loan officer, the real estate agent needs to have some type of communication system in place. You need to be able to contact them and know that if they are not available at the time of your call they will be calling you within the next 30 minutes or so. Most agents can be contacted by office phone, cell phone, email, or even text messages. It is very important to know what that mode of communication is for that agent.

It is also important to know that the agent is working for a reputable broker. I am not saying that only big firms can provide good service but it is important to know that if something happens during the contract negotiations that particular agent has the backing of a stable real estate firm. You have to remember this is a business transaction and anything can happen when dealing with such a large transaction. That is why it is important to have an agent especially if you have not purchased a home before. You can meet some people who are not working with the best morals and get you into a deal that is not so good.

An agent's job is to represent you during this transaction. That is why it is important for them to know what it is that you truly want as well as know what you can afford to purchase. They need to be able to negotiate with the seller or seller's agent the terms that will satisfy your wants and needs. A good agent can make a deal run smoothly when otherwise it would have been a train wreck. A good agent can not only find you the house you want but negotiate a great price for it as well as have the seller pay the closing costs. A good agent is definitely worth their weight in gold. That is why the interview is such an important process.

I cannot emphasize enough the importance of a good real estate agent especially if you are purchasing your first home. This process can be very intimidating and you need people around you who are experienced, knowledgeable, and tenacious. You need to know that they got your back. Now since I am a loan officer I feel as though my job is the most important and of course, the real estate agent feels the same. This is why we sometimes do not get along. We both feel as though we do not need the other when in actuality we do both need each other to make the process run smoothly.

The search for your home can be a grueling process. A good real estate agent can make this process a lot less painful. As I am writing this book, the country is currently experiencing a housing crisis. Home foreclosures are at a record level. Although the market is down it is actually a great time to purchase a home. This is what is considered a "buyer's market" in which it is a better situation for the buyers than for the sellers.

In a buyer's market, the sellers are more likely to offer more concessions to the buyer meaning they will usually accept a lesser offer from the buyer. They will probably be willing to assist with the closing costs, which will help the purchaser save thousands of dollars. Now this can also happen in a "seller's market" but a seller is usually motivated to accommodate most demands from a buyer when their house has been on the market for over a year.

The search for your home can take several months so you should prepare yourself for that. I suggest you sit down and determine what type of house you are looking for. The problem most people have is when this is their first home purchase they usually get frustrated with the time frame and settle for something other than what they really want. I feel this is a bad idea especially when you are paying a large sum of money such as a mortgage. You should decide in your mind what you want and what you will settle for and stick to it.

While going through this process of locating your new home make sure you look at more than the cosmetics of the home. What I am saying is do not get so caught up with just the looks of the property. Although that is very important, what is more important is the functionality of the home. Let me give you an example. I had a client who was purchasing her first home. She was a single mom with two children and very excited about buying her first home. She had recently divorced her husband and this was part of her statement of independence.

Well she went through the process with me and got pre-approved and I gave her a pre-approval letter. I connected her with a real estate agent from a reputable real estate agency and they searched for a home. I told her the same thing I am telling you. I told her not to get caught up so much in the looks of the home and to make sure that it functions properly. I told her to have a home inspection done in which a professional inspects the home to make sure the major components work properly. The inspector will check the roof, the foundation, the heating and air conditioning units, the plumbing and other major components.

Instead, she listened to her sister and decided not to have an inspection done. She felt that any house that looked as good as this particular property did could not have any problems with it. She went against the advice of the real estate agent and me. Therefore, we closed on the house and she moved in excitedly. Well a few months later she found out that the roof was leaking, the air conditioning unit needed to be replaced, as well as there were problems with the plumbing in the kitchen. You see when you are buying a house there is no maintenance man to call to fix things like this. You have to fix these problems yourself and they can be very expensive. There are home warranties available for some homes but these are usually new homes. If you have an older home then you probably will not have a warranty, as was the case for my client.

It took her several months to fix the problems in her new home, which meant she had to suffer through the time of dealing with these problems. She later told me that it really put a damper on the excitement of her new home purchase. She said it was hard being excited about her new home when every time it rained she had to get buckets out to catch the leaks in her house. She told me that she wished she had taken my advice and gotten that home inspection. If she would've had the inspection done and these issues were discovered before closing then it would have been the seller's responsibility to fix them, which would have saved the buyer a lot of heartache and money.

Again, I cannot emphasize enough that this is a process in which you need to make a careful and educated selection. I have seen it repeatedly when someone lets their emotions get the best of them and think they are buying a dream home only to find out that it is a nightmare.

Now that you have selected the house that you would like to purchase, your real estate agent contacts the seller with a contract offer. Depending on the situation of the sale, your agent will make an offer either at the sale price or below. They will also ask for certain amenities such as closing cost assistance or decorating allowances. In a buyer's market, the purchaser has a good chance of receiving amenities from the seller. It is not out of the question to get closing cost assistance, decorating allowance, as well as down payment assistance.

A seller is motivated to do whatever they have to do in order to sell their house when the market is slow. Imagine being in a situation where you have to move to a new location because of your job. So now, you have a new house but still have a mortgage payment at the previous location. Therefore, you put your house up for sale but it takes over a year to sell. You have to pay that mortgage payment until that house sells so now you are paying two mortgages. You are motivated to sell this house because those two mortgage payments are kicking your butt.

A motivated seller can be a tremendous blessing to a buyer. They can make the deal close when it may not otherwise be possible. I have seen deals where a seller was willing to hold a second mortgage in order to provide the down payment needed to close the deal. I have also seen deals where the seller gives the buyer a two-year grace period before having to make the first payment on that second mortgage with no interest accruing during that time. I have also seen deals where the seller completely forgives the debt of the second mortgage and tears it up.

You may wonder again, why the seller would forgive the buyer's debt of the second mortgage. Let's say the seller is selling his house for $200,000. The buyer qualifies for a 90% percent loan amount of $180,000. Therefore, they need $20,000 for a down payment but they do not have it. The seller is willing to hold a second mortgage of $20,000 in order to close the deal. They may only owe $80,000 on the house so they will still walk away with close to $100,000 after paying closing costs. This way they have gotten rid of the second mortgage payment and put a lot of money in the bank as well. Therefore, this is a win-win scenario for everyone.

Once the two parties have come to an agreement on the contract price and details then the second part of the process begins. You will be expected to give a deposit with the contract, which could range from $500-$5000 or more depending on the amount of the contract. This is called Earnest Money. The purpose of this is to protect the seller just in case you decide you do not want to purchase the property. In that case, your deposit is non-refundable. You may feel that a deposit should not be necessary but once you have placed a contract on the property the seller cannot technically entertain any other offers, which mean they have taken their property off the market. Therefore, it is not fair to them to miss a potential buyer hoping you will purchase it only to have you pull out of the deal. This happens often.

Next, the loan officer will order an appraisal, title work, and probably an inspection of the property. All of these are necessary to bring this transaction to a close. An appraisal is necessary to make sure that the property is worth what you are paying for it. In addition, the lender wants to make sure of this as well since they are lending you the funds to purchase the property. They are not going to lend you an amount that is more than what the property is worth. In addition, an appraisal can be affected by several factors. It is not just what you think the property is worth or even what the property was worth at an earlier date. One of the main factors that affect the value of a property is what similar properties in that area are selling for. This is referred to as comparable sales.

The "comps" always have a drastic effect on the appraisal. I have had properties that were worth one amount but because there were no current comparable sales that could support that amount, the lender reduced the amount significantly. In addition, the comps have to be within a close proximity to the property you are purchasing usually within a mile. This means an appraiser cannot go to another city for instance and find a property to support the value they are seeking. The comparable sales also need to have sold within a certain time frame, usually 3-12 months depending on current trends in the area.

Another factor that effects an appraisal is the condition of the property. If there are majors items that need to be repaired such as the roof, no heat or air conditioning, plumbing is extremely old, floors are rotting out, rooms with walls that are not complete. These things can reduce the value of a property significantly. A good appraiser is a valuable asset to the loan process. He can sometimes make or break a deal. The loan officer should know the value of an appraiser and pick them very wisely.

Another important factor to the purchase is the title search of the property. A title search is when a title company or real estate attorney enlists a person to research the history of the subject property. They contact the city/county real estate assessor's office to inquire about the ownership history of the property. They then check to see if there are any liens against the property. This is extremely important because if a creditor has placed a lien against a property and you purchase that property without first researching the title, that creditor's lien is still in effect. Meaning they have a right to come and possess the house, you are staying in, in order to sell it for the amount that is owed to them.

A title company will research this for you and then offer you owner's insurance to cover you in the case they were not able to find a lien against the property and there was still one in existence. The insurance will cover you in that case and pay off the lien so that the creditor cannot take your house. A title company will also research your credit and the seller's credit to make sure there are no judgments against either of you. They do this because by law they are supposed to take any proceeds due to either of you and pay off those judgments. In addition, the title company makes sure that at the closing, whoever is suppose to receive a check from the transaction, receives those funds in either a wire transfer or cashier's check.

They also follow the instructions of the lender pertaining to the transaction. They make sure all funds that are supposed to be received at closing are received in the proper manner. They also go over the details of the transaction so that both parties understand fully. It is still the responsibility of both the seller and buyer to ask any questions that they may have.

When you finally reach the closing table, you should already have an understanding of what to expect. You should know where to go and what to bring with you. For most closings, you are required to go to the closing attorney's office or maybe a title company. You can also have your closing done at your home; it depends upon the title company's capabilities. You will need some identification and if you are required to bring settlement fees then they must be in the form of a cashier's check.

For a purchase closing, the sellers and purchasers are required to attend because both parties are required to sign the settlement documents. Normally the real estate agents will be in attendance as well as the loan officers. It is not necessarily required that the loan officer attend the closing. They usually attend just in case something goes wrong during the closing.

Let's say the closing documents arrive from the lender with different terms listed on them. This is why I require the closing attorney or title company to fax over the HUD-1, which is the final settlement statement, for me to review before the closing. This gives me the opportunity to address any potential problems before the closing thus avoiding any delay of the closing.

Now let me address something about this entire loan process. People need to understand that there are a number of people that are involved in a closing. You have the loan officer, real estate agent, underwriter, closing department, funding department, title agents, closing attorneys, and maybe a few others. That means there are plenty of opportunities for someone to make a mistake. That is why the loan officer makes sure his portion is correct and the real estate agent makes sure their portion is correct as well as the closing attorney.

While everyone is attempting to work as professionally as possible, things can still happen to cause delays in the process. The problem is this is the largest financial obligation that most people will ever partake in and to be honest it can become very nerve wracking. We understand the anxiety that people experience but that is why you interview and carefully select your loan officer and real estate agent so that they can relieve you of the majority of that stress but you have to allow them to do their jobs.

While I am on this topic; let me delve into it a little deeper. People have a tendency to do one of two things when issues arise during a closing. Either they lose all trust in their main two components i.e. loan officer and real estate agent or they completely trust them without question. I do not recommend you make either of those choices.

When the client loses all trust in their main two components, they start asking other people about their closings and soliciting their opinions. That is when I hear, "My brother said his closing didn't go like this. He said that you must don't know what you are doing." Or "My sister's boyfriend's cousin is a loan officer and he said that this should never happen." Now when I initially hear these complaints I want to respond by saying, "Well your sister's boyfriend's cousin should have done your loan"; but of course I do not say that because I am a professional.

Now the other situation is when you completely trust your main two components without asking any questions. I know you are saying that I just said I should trust them but now I am saying not to trust them. What I am saying is to trust in the abilities of your main two components but do not be afraid to ask questions. There is a difference between asking questions and criticizing a person. No one wants to be criticized by anyone but everyone has the right to question.

The reason I am saying this is why I feel the problems occur with a person not knowing what type of loan they have. When I hear people say that they did not know they had an adjustable rate loan it is really disturbing to me. Because when you are at a closing and you are in the midst of signing the vast amount of paperwork required to finalize a deal, you realize why the previous statement disturbs me. There are so many documents in a closing package that PLAINLY state what type of loan you are agreeing to. There is no way someone cannot know what type of loan they have when there are at least a dozen or more papers which state the type of loan and the terms of that loan in plain English.

I have attended dozens of closings in which the clients never read any of the paperwork they are signing. I have interrupted the closing and pointed out to the client the importance of reading the paperwork they are signing. Most clients will say that they are reading it but I know they are not unless they are experienced speed-readers. Other clients will just say, "I trust you" in which I always respond to them with this statement, "I DO NOT WANT YOU TO TRUST ME WITH THIS TRANSACTION. PLEASE READ ALL OF THE PAPERWORK."

Again, I understand in a way why a person would not want to take the time to read everything. One reason is they are usually so excited about being at the closing after a lengthy process so they just want to get it over with and get the keys to the house or the check from the transaction. Another reason is it is a lot of paperwork. Most closing packages can be between 75 to a 100 pages. The average person takes several months to read a 100-page book so to ask them to do that in a couple of hours is asking a lot. Again, I have to say that this is the most important financial transaction that the average person will ever encounter so for that reason alone everyone needs to take the time and read the paperwork and ask questions.

The last reason people do not want to read the paperwork is they fear that there will be something they will not understand and they do not want to feel ignorant. First of all, there is nothing wrong with being ignorant about a particular subject. The definition of ignorance according to Webster's dictionary is, *"lacking knowledge or the comprehension of things specified."* Everyone is ignorant about something. No one knows everything although there are some who think they do.

The problem occurs when a person allows their ignorance to produce fear, which hinders them from learning. In this instance, it places a person in a position where they need to ask questions in order to obtain a full understanding of what they are agreeing to especially when it is a large financial obligation.

This is why it really upsets me to hear so many people on the news state that they did not know what type of loan they were agreeing to when they obtained their mortgage. This was the cause of the "sub-prime mortgage crisis." Our country always feels a need to blame someone or something when a so call crisis occurs. So as usual, the loan officer was to blame for not explaining to them what type of loan they had.

This reminds me of a person buying a car for what seems to be a "great" deal. My grandfather used to say, "When something seems too good to be true, it usually is." A man agrees to buy a car for a great price. He never asks the salesman why the price of the car is so cheap. He never has a mechanic look at the car to check for any potential problems. He never asks about the history of the car. He is only focused on the "great" price of the car.

Therefore, the buyer pays for the car and leaves with the car. The car drives fine for a few weeks but then there seems to be a problem. He hears a loud knocking noise from under the hood and sees smoke. Well the first thing he does is call the salesman who sold him the car. The salesman immediately reminds him that the sale was an "as-is" sale, which means there is no warranty on the car. The buyer gets upset and starts ranting and raving about how the guy sold him a bad car. Well the buyer's father asks him if he had a mechanic look at the car before purchasing it. He also asks if the buyer asked about the history of the car. The buyer answers no to both questions but continues to complain about getting a raw deal. The father calmly looks at the son and tells him that when you enter into a financial agreement with another person you must first do your "due diligence" in order to protect your end of the transaction. He also told him that if he would have had a mechanic to look at the car before buying it he probably would have found out what was wrong with the vehicle. Lastly, he stated that when you are getting a deal that seems too good to be true you must research everything about that deal before agreeing to it to find out why are they offering this deal with those terms.

That story is the same situation that millions encountered during the "refinance boom." This was the period when millions agreed to mortgages with terms that were "too good to be true." People agreed to mortgages with ridiculously low interest rates in the beginning of the mortgage for a short period of time like 2,3,5, or 10 years. This allowed them to qualify for homes that they actually could not afford. Therefore, when the "starter periods" ended and the real interest rates and terms kicked in, they found themselves with a mortgage payment they could not afford.

Before you knew it, millions had mortgages that they could not afford and the country found themselves in a crisis because foreclosures were out of control and the lenders had all of these homes that they had to take back from the clients. So now, you had all these people crying foul claiming they did not know they had an adjustable rate mortgage. That is an example of how our society likes to pass blame onto someone else. No one wants to own up to his or her responsibility. When it all comes down to it, you are an adult and responsible for anything you put your signature on. If you do not understand what you are agreeing to then DO NOT SIGN THE AGREEMENT.

I have a radio show that I host called, "On the Couch with the Mortgage Therapist." I made the same statement I just made about being responsible for what you sign and a woman called into my show. She was very irate. She stated that she had an adjustable rate mortgage and she did not know what she was doing when she signed the papers. She stated that she felt it was the loan officer's job to make sure she knew what type of loan she had. She refused to take any responsibility for agreeing to that loan.

I asked her did the loan officer ever tell her that she had an adjustable rate mortgage. She said that she could not remember. I asked her if she remembered during her closing if the attorney explained to her that she was agreeing to an adjustable rate mortgage. Again, she stated that she could not remember. I asked her one more question. Did she still have her settlement papers that the title company gave her after closing? She said she did and went to find them. I kept her on hold because this was good banter for my show. When she returned to the phone, she was all excited because she did find her papers and she was determined to prove to me that the paperwork did not say anything about adjustable rates.

There was a pause on the phone and then she started claiming that her papers must have been switched. I asked her what her paperwork stated and she agreed that it stated in bold letters "ADJUSTABLE RATE MORTGAGE" on at least eight pages in her package. She began to rant that they must have switched her paperwork because she would have noticed that. I asked her lastly to locate the copy of her application that was taken by her loan officer, which was in that package as well. When she found it I asked her what was checked on the first page pertaining to whether her rate would be fixed or ARM. She informed me that it stated ARM, which stands for adjustable rate mortgage.

She continued to insist that although she had signed over 10 pages between her application and the settlement documents, which clearly stated that her loan would be an adjustable rate mortgage, that it still was the loan officer's responsibility to make sure she understood. I asked her if after signing all those pages, which did state that fact and not asking one question about her loan terms, that maybe, just maybe, her loan officer assumed she understood. She did not respond to that statement. She just hung up the phone.

The reason I told that story was to reiterate that people must always understand what they are agreeing to in a contract. A mortgage is a contractual agreement between you and the lender that you will pay back the loan they have issued on your behalf under the specific terms of that agreement. If there is anything in that agreement you may not understand you must first obtain a clear understanding before signing that agreement. If you do not get that understanding and sign the agreement anyway, then you are responsible for upholding the terms regardless of your understanding of them. You cannot cry foul after the fact. You should have done your due diligence before agreeing to it.

As you can tell this is a sensitive subject for me. Everyday all you saw on the news was about predatory lenders. How the mortgage companies were taking advantage of their clients by giving them mortgages with outrageous terms. The lenders would not have been able to loan the money to people if we as a society were not so credit driven and money greedy. Anyway, I said all of that to say this. Make sure you completely understand the terms of your mortgage before agreeing and signing any papers. Do not give away your responsibility to the loan officer or real estate agent. They are not going to pay your mortgage for you. You are the only one responsible for that mortgage.

Okay now that you have read all of the papers in your closing package and signed all of the necessary papers, the moment you have waited for comes. The closing agent hands you the keys to your new home. This is one of those great moments in your life. It is similar to your wedding day, the birth of a child, graduation from school, etc. I do not care how many times it happens. It still is a great feeling to hold the keys to a new property. The realization that you are now a homeowner is a great feeling. You have just joined the team. Now the real fun begins.

Part Four

Becoming a Player

"Take the first step in faith. You don't have to see the whole staircase, just take the first step."

Martin Luther King, Jr.

Now that you have joined the team of homeownership, let us not get comfortable. Remember the focus of this book is to use homeownership to establish financial stability. This is how you can become a player in this economic game of life. The main purpose of focusing on becoming a homeowner to establish yourself financially is because it helps you build wealth.

Wealth is what is needed to stabilize your finances. According to Webster's dictionary, wealth is an abundance of valuable material possessions. It is what differentiates one economic class from the next. The difference between a rich person and a wealthy person is a rich person is someone with a substantial income. A wealthy person is someone who has valuable possessions, which create an income in itself. As long as that wealthy person owns those possessions then their income will not only sustain but also probably increase.

I saw comedian Chris Rock perform on television once and he spoke on the difference between a wealthy person and a rich person. He said, "Basketball All-Star Shaquille O'Neal is rich. The person who signs his paycheck is wealthy. He said Oprah is rich but Bill Gates is wealthy." A wealthy person's resources affect other persons' income.

A rich person has to continue to produce that income in order to sustain this status. A wealthy person's status is based and sustained by other factors than just income. A verse in the bible states the importance of a person obtaining wealth. It is Proverbs 13:22.

"A good man leaveth an inheritance to his children's children:"

In order for someone to be in position to leave anything to not just their children but also their children's children, they must have "an abundance of valuable material possessions." For the majority of people, we don't have a lot of valuable possessions. Most of us do not have stocks and bonds. We do not own valuable jewelry or property. For the average person our wealth usually starts with a home.

Most of us know someone whose father or grandfather left them a house or some land. This was the norm for previous generations especially in the minority communities. The reason for this was most people worked to own their homes and the land the home was on. They understood the importance of purchasing something that they could actually call their own. Something they could eventually give to their children and maybe even their grandchildren. Those generations were not credit driven and money greedy. In fact, they did not like dealing with credit at all. They believed in saving up to buy something. I can remember my grandfather saying that if you cannot pay cash for it then you do not need it.

I can remember he had one of the first charge cards available. It was a Master Charge. I remember when I was ten years old and first started playing football. I needed some equipment to play recreation league football. I needed a helmet, shoulder pads, a pair of pants, and some cleats. My mother did not have the money to pay for it and since she really did not want me to play football anyway would not have paid for it if she had the money. My father was missing in action at the time, so my mother told me to ask my grandfather. I called him and asked him for the money and after a small lecture on being responsible for something that someone has given you he agreed to buy the equipment.

He took me to Harrell's Sporting Goods in Portsmouth, VA. I can remember it like it was yesterday. After I told the man everything I needed and he rang it up on the cash register, my grandfather pulled out his charge card to pay for it. That really amazed me that you could buy something and pay for it with a plastic card. I told my grandfather that I wish I had one of those cards. He told me that you should be careful using a charge card and to only use it if you can pay it off at the end of the month.

My grandfather was from a generation where they valued money and their reputation. They understood how hard it was for someone, especially a minority, to obtain any type of property of their own. They cherished what they owned and took pride in paying for it with their own money. I can remember my grandfather telling me that a man should always take care of his family while he is living and after he is gone. I never knew what he meant by "after he is gone." Nevertheless, what he was referring to was leaving an inheritance for your children.

Let us dwell on this a little more. The purpose of leaving wealth for your children is to give them a leg up, a boost so to speak, on life. It allows them to have a chance of surviving life's tough times. I think we have lost the true meaning of raising a family. Raising a child does not stop when that child reaches the legal age of eighteen. When a parent takes on the responsibility of raising a child that continues until that child is able to take care of themselves and essentially raise a family of their own.

My grandfather left my mother a house that was paid off. That gave her an asset that she was able to use in her time of need. When my parents divorced, my mother left my father and basically had to start from scratch. She was employed but her income was not strong enough to make a decent living off. The value of the house that was left to her gave her options. It primarily allowed her to have a place for her and her children to live with no rent or mortgage payment to be paid. She was able to use the equity in the house and access it in order to pay certain financial obligations that she had.

I feel that our generation has been a little selfish. I feel that we have been so caught up in "keeping up with the Joneses" that we forgot our true purpose as parents. That purpose is to raise responsible children who in turn become responsible adults. A responsible person is one who respects others by being a good citizen in their community and contributing to the betterment of society. That means they do not take from society they contribute to the good of society.

When a person is financially stable, they are in position to contribute to the success of the community and thus society. They are able to donate to charity. They are able to provide an education for their children so that they are in position to do the same. It becomes a cycle when the financial foundation is stable in a family. Certain things are expected from family members when finances are not a major problem.

I can remember looking at an interview of Maria Shriver. You may know Maria Shriver as the wife of Arnold Schwarzenegger, the famous movie actor and once

Governor of California. However, Maria definitely had made a name for herself prior to meeting the actor/governor. She was a successful journalist and even before that, she was a part of the famous Kennedy clan. Her mother Eunice was the sister of the late President John F Kennedy.

Anyway, during the interview, she was asked about how it was to grow up in the Kennedy family. She stated that certain things were expected of the children. That it was expected of each person to excel in school. It was expected of them to have a goal, cause, or project that they were working on that gave back to the community. They were expected to remember that it is important to "give" to those in need. She stated that this was an expectation of everyone within their family both immediate and extended families.

This seemed very interesting to me because the main factor in that story was that the family had the means so that the children were able to pursue certain goals and causes. Now I am sure you know that the Kennedy's have been one of the wealthiest families in the history of this country. The patriarch Joseph P. Kennedy created the family's wealth. The elder Kennedy was the son a saloonkeeper in the late 1800's, who attended Harvard University. He had some legitimate businesses but many historians agree that he made his fortune by running liquor from Europe during Prohibition. By the 1930's, he had made enough money to focus solely on his legitimate businesses.

This man had enough sense to use his ill-gotten fortune to establish a financial foundation that lasted over four generations and counting. He understood the responsibilities of raising a family. He realized that it meant more than just helping your kids finish high school and then they are on their own. He grasped the concept of laying a path for your children to run on. Unlike the Kennedy's, most families have to focus on basic survival. Keeping a roof over their heads and food on the table are accomplishments in themselves. Nevertheless, imagine just imagine how life would be different if that basic struggle was eliminated. You too could teach your children to focus on contributing to society.

This leads me back to the purpose of this section. Now that you have purchased that home, let us use it for what it is supposed to be used for. There are many advantages to being a homeowner such as tax write offs and equity build-ups. Let us focus on tax write offs first.

In the U.S., a person can take the amount of interest paid on a mortgage and use as a deduction on their taxes. That is a significant amount of money. Imagine what you currently get back on your tax return. Most of us know exactly what to expect on our tax return because we look forward to that time every year. Okay now add an additional several thousand dollars to that amount depending on your mortgage. That changes tax return time significantly. For instance instead of getting back $4,000-5,000 on your return you get back $7,000-10,000. Check with your tax advisor for exact amounts but either way it is significant.

Let's say that your tax return increases by an additional $4,000 a year. This does not mean its "Party Time." It means now you have resources that you can use to pay off credit bills, pay down your mortgage faster, or maybe just create a savings. Over 70% of Americans do not have a significant savings account, which could be used in times of emergency. I know my wife and I were in our late thirties before we had a savings account. It makes a big difference to have access to resources that can be used in tough times.

That addition to your tax return changes many things. It contributes to the financial foundation that you are establishing. However, if used recklessly it can contribute to your downfall financially. We must remember what was discussed in an earlier chapter dealing with having a budget. This budget is as important if not more important after purchasing a home than it was before getting the house.

The next major benefit of homeownership is accessing the equity in your home. Let me first explain the term equity. The dictionary defines equity as "the monetary value of a property or business beyond any amounts owed on it in mortgages, claims, or liens." In layman's terms, it means if your house is valued at $200,000 but you only owe $80,000 on your mortgage then you have $120,000 worth of equity in your home.

Now because the house's title is in your name that means you can access that $120,000. At this point, that equity is wealth for you because it sustains itself and can increase over time. Now because of what happened during the mortgage crisis when the property values declined drastically people actually loss that value which in turn meant they loss that wealth. There are people who because of that believe homeownership is not stable. They believe that owning a home is a bad investment. I disagree with that belief.

Every investment whether it is in the stock market or real estate or a business has the chance of losing money. There is no guaranteed "No Lose" investment no matter what some people may say. Even so, I feel that real estate especially your personal real estate is the best investment a person can have. Now let us get back to that equity that I mentioned.

Therefore, you have access to $120,000 worth of equity in your house. Most lenders will allow you to borrow against the value of your property but they do not want you to exhaust all of the value, which means you will not be able to get a loan for the entire $120,000. They will allow you to have a lien equal to 80% of the value so since the value is $200,000 you can have a lien equal to $160,000. You already owe $80,000 on your mortgage so you can get another $80,000 in cash.

That is a lot of money for anyone to have at one time. A person can do a lot of different things with that amount of money. The problem that a lot of Americans have is we use this money for the wrong things. We purchase new vehicles. Take extravagant vacations or purchase other things such as jewelry or clothing that we may consider valuable, which actually are not. These things are all bad choices and move us in the wrong direction financially.

One of the things we could use the money for is to pay off other debts so that the only bill we have is our mortgage payment. That is called a debt consolidation loan, which allows you to simplify things by grouping all your bills into one payment. This is one of the smartest moves anyone can make financially. It is usually at a lower interest rate than what we were paying with the separate bills that we had before and it allows us to stay in control of our finances.

Other people may take that equity and use it to pay for their children's education whether its private schooling or even college. This way allows your children to obtain a college education and not have to obtain a large amount of student loans which they would be paying on for many years after school thus again giving them a step up in life. That is the true meaning of the biblical verse Proverbs 13:22 leaving an inheritance to your children. You are making life better for them than it was for you.

One thing that the money could be used for is to create a business. I have helped individuals take their equity money to invest in a small business. Something they have wanted to do for a while but did not have the startup capital. I have helped families start daycares because they just had a child and did not want the wife to go back to work. Therefore, they used the equity to start a daycare in order for the wife to be home with the child and create a decent income. The majority of the time they actually exceeded her job income with the daycare income.

I've also helped families start other small businesses such as landscaping, computer technical support, hot dog stand, automotive repair shop, printing shop, photography business, and catering business just to name a few. These families utilized the equity from their homes to create a productive and positive income. The majority of which eventually became their main incomes.

In these instances, they did something positive with the money.

Another thing I have assisted people with was real estate investment. This was a very popular opportunity before the mortgage crisis and believe it or not, it still is a great opportunity. You see all the time on television the commercials advertising flipping houses. They always have a so-called expert telling about how successful they were in the real estate investment business. They always speak about the "no money down" opportunities.

In the late '90s and early 2000s there were plenty of "no money down" opportunities but after the mortgage plunge those opportunities have disappeared. Now, are there instances where a person can basically walk into a deal with little money out of their pockets? Yes, there are still opportunities like that but they are hard to come by especially if any bank financing is needed.

What I mean by that is there was a time when I could purchase a property from a seller. The bank would give me an 85% loan on the property and allow the seller to hold a second loan for the remaining 15% of the selling price. Then the seller would also pay all closing costs on the property as well. After the closing of the house, the seller would forgive me of the second loan thus leaving me to have to pay nothing out of my pocket. I did plenty of loans like this during the so-called mortgage boom. We did 2-3 deals a month like this.

I mentioned a similar scenario earlier in this book and it was a win-win situation for all parties. The seller was usually selling a house in which there was a ton of equity in it so for him to settle for 85% of the sale price was usually a huge profit on his part. Now the only way a deal could go down this way was if the owner was financing the deal himself or herself. Owner financing is when the owner owns the property outright and agrees to accept monthly payments from the buyer. Very rarely do you ever see this scenario though without a significant down payment from the buyer.

Anyway, let us get back to the subject of investment property purchasing. I can remember helping a young gentleman nearly ten years ago become a real estate investor. He contacted me because his mother had passed and left him her house. The house was paid for with no liens on it at all. I was able to secure an equity line of credit for him with the house as collateral in the amount of $85,000. He wanted to invest in his friend's music career and build a studio.

I could tell that he was really uneasy about spending the money on the studio when he first shared the ideal with me. After I met his friend and heard him sing I could understand why he was hesitant. His friend's musical abilities were elementary at best and that is saying it nicely. Let the truth be told he was awful and after this man kept asking me my opinion on his friend's singing, I finally told him so. I told him there was no way in hell I would spend a dime on this guy especially not a dime that came from the house his late mother had sacrificed to purchase as a single mother and left for him to take care of.

Therefore, he asked me what else he could do with the money. He was not interested in going to school to get another degree. He had already finished college and gotten his bachelor's degree. That was a struggle to accomplish that and he was not interested in enduring any more of that kind of pain. He also knew that if he did not do something with the money that his family would be coming with their hands out begging for some of it. "Mr. Clifton I just want to do something with this money that would make my mother proud," he told me.

I suggested that he purchase some investment property. I explained to him how he could hire a contractor to fix the property up and either rent them out or sell them for a profit. We sat down and devised a business plan detailing each step that would be needed to make this venture profitable. I connected him with some trust worthy real estate agents as well as contractors. Those are two of the three key parts every person will need to be successful in real estate investment.

You need a good real estate agent to find the right type of properties in the right neighborhoods. Then you need a good contractor. One who will show up to work when they say they will. One who will tell you a price and stick to that price. One who you can trust around your property and not have to worry about them giving you a quality performance. Lastly, you need a good mortgage loan officer who knows how to originate an investment deal. These deals are not the same as regular owner-occupied loans. A good loan officer is worth their weight in gold for a real estate investor. I know because I was that loan officer for many years and I made many investors really happy because I helped them make a lot of money.

Now back to my guy. After we devised a business plan, we purchased a nice duplex, which consisted of two two-bedroom apartments. It was sold for back taxes to the city only, so he got it at $45,000 below city-assessed value. So at the AS-IS condition he had already made a $45,000 profit at the city-assessed value, which is usually below the actual appraised value. When I explained this to him, he was extremely happy.

The property needed some structural work done to it such as securing the foundation around the property, new windows, new floors in both units, a new roof, aluminum siding for the entire property, and new HVAC units for both units. Then there were cosmetic work needed such as kitchen cabinets, carpeting, bathroom tub and toilets, kitchen appliances, as well as painting the inside of both units.

The contractor gave him a good price on the work because we explained to him what his business plan was and told him that if he did well on this first project he would be the primary contractor on all of the future projects as well. It took the contractor less than a month to complete all of the work. Once he was finished I had an appraiser come out and give him a full appraisal of the property. When the appraisal came back, my guy's property had increased by an additional $60,000. Now remember he purchased the property at $45,000 under the city assessment value. The appraised value gave him a total of $105,000 worth of equity for the property. My guy was a really happy camper at this point.

He decided that he wanted to rent out the property and was able to get $900 per month per unit. I then helped him refinance the property and pull out some of the equity that was in it so that he could recoup the amount that he used to pay for the property and receive an additional

$25,000. He used some of the rent money that he was receiving from his two renters to pay the loan amount and he pocketed the rest.

At that moment, I had created a monster. When he really saw what his potentials were he attacked the investment market like a mad man. He began looking for potential properties to purchase himself. He continued to use the real estate agent but after a while, he became an expert at it himself. During the first year, he purchased three units in which he rehabbed them and either sold them or rented them out. The next year he bought an additional five units but only sold one of them. The third year I helped him purchase two four-unit apartment complexes and five single family homes in which he kept all of them.

By his fourth year, my guy had built his portfolio up to 15 single-family homes, five four-unit apartments, and an eight-unit apartment building. He was receiving nearly $8,000 per month in profit, which more than exceeded his job pay at the shipyard. His net wealth was valued at over $2 million at that point. I remember one day he came over to my house and we were sitting in my office. We were discussing a potential deal and all of a sudden, I started laughing. Right at that moment, I was reminded of when I had first met him and he was a shy, nervous, average guy. He drove an old Honda Accord, which leaked oil, and the belts were squealing on it. He was staying in a one-bedroom apartment living paycheck to paycheck. At that moment, I was looking at a strong, positive, confident man. He had pulled up to my house in a Cadillac Escalade truck which he had paid cash for and he was living in a four-bedroom house with his wife and child which was valued at over $400,000. It was amazing how much his life had changed in just four years.

Now I am telling you this not to create a pipe dream for you. Was it easy for him to build his value to over $2 million? No, there were many obstacles he had to endure and overcome. Can anyone do this? Yes if you are willing and disciplined. He was a sponge. He soaked up any and everything I said to him. He was determined to learn and succeed at this business. He decided early on that he was going to use the gift that his mother left for him in order to improve his lifestyle and the lifestyle of his family. I think his mother would have been extremely proud of what he did with what she left him.

Now I have plenty of stories not necessarily to that extreme but many in which people used their equity and purchased investment property. Some bought small single-family homes and kept them for rental property. Some bought large multi-family properties and created a nice income. Some used their equity to purchase small homes for their children as wedding gifts. I cannot think of a better wedding gift than a small starter home for your kids. I think it is a better use of money than to spend it on an expensive wedding. But that's just my opinion.

<u>Conclusion</u>

"Those who have the most wealth and the most property, their children have The First, The Best, and The Most."

Jesse Jackson

Let us summarize what we have discussed in this book. We have talked mainly about money and how we handle our money. I shared with you the mistakes I made with my money early on and to be honest even sometimes now. This is an ongoing process in which you have to fight to stay discipline with your money. You can do well with managing your money for months and even years and fall into a bad period in which you make some dumb decisions that affect your money in a negative way. I am here to tell you that if and when that happens you are not alone and although it may be frustrating, you can regroup and get back on track to good money management.

We discussed having a budget. I cannot stress strongly and loudly enough how important a budget is to your family. This is and will continue to be the most difficult thing for you to stay disciplined with. A budget allows you to stay on top of things financially but it is the easiest thing to move away from. It is easy to stay on track when money is tight the problems occur when you have a little extra. That is when you want to splurge and do some things you feel you deserve, when in actuality this is the time that you need to stay on your budget the most. But again let me tell you that we all fall short in this department so when it happens to you do not get frustrated just refocus and get back on track.

We discussed dealing with our credit. I explained and suggested some ways to improve your credit. I did not suggest any quick credit repair techniques because I believe we need to diligently work on our credit. We did not destroy it overnight so we should not expect to repair it overnight. For most of us if we were able to repair our credit quickly, we would just quickly mess it up again. That has a lot of truth to it. Most of us do not deserve to have our credit fixed fast. We need to discipline ourselves and develop proper financial habits.

We talked about the process of finding a home as well as finding a loan officer for the mortgage. Remember that although it seems like you are in the begging stage because you are hoping that they will give you the loan, in actuality you are in charge. Let me say that again, YOU ARE IN CHARGE. You are the one who has to pay that mortgage for 15, 20, or 30 years with your money. Therefore, because of that you are the one who decides how it should go. Do not allow anyone to bully you into an agreement that you first do not understand or especially do not agree with.

Remember what I said, it does not matter what anyone says when it comes down to it you are the only one responsible for the loan you agreed to by signing your name. If you do not understand something, ASK A QUESTION. If something feels wrong, ASK A QUESTION. If you feel rushed or pressured by the real estate agent, the loan officer, the seller, or even your spouse, take a moment and regroup. It will be hard to do this because you are so close when it has been a while to get to that point but if you are not comfortable then back away for a moment. It is better to be safe than sorry. Do not commit yourself to something you are not sure you can handle. Do not be afraid to walk away.

We also talked about what happens after you have purchased the house. The opportunities that come along with owning a home. The tax benefits and the equity build-up. The possibilities that present themselves that you can use the equity for. The consolidation of debt; paying for your child's education; starting a small business; and purchasing investment property.

I initially wrote this book focusing on minorities. My intentions were to detail how a strong financial foundation could be built through homeownership. I hope I have not only shown minorities such as African Americans and Hispanics but also anyone who is not a homeowner. Homeownership for the average American whether they are black, white, Hispanic, or any other ethnic group can assist you in lifting your family to a new and stable financial foundation.

JOIN THE MOVEMENT

The Mortgage Therapist has committed to assist 1,000 people become first-time homebuyers. He is willing to work with individuals and couples in every aspect from credit repair, budgeting, down payment assistance as well as loan qualifications.

Mortgage Therapist Coaching Program:

$25 per month:

- **Receive one on one coaching to prepare your credit**

- **Receive a monthly newsletter**

- **Receive budget assistance**

- **Free loan qualification**

- **Free home inspection**

- **Home warming gift after closing**

Go to www.davianclifton.com to sign up for the coaching program or call 1-888-557-7218

Tune into one of the hottest radio shows "On the couch with the Mortgage Therapist" every Monday at 5 pm on BlogtalkRadio.com at www.blogtalkradio.com/mortgage-therapist

- Author Davian Clifton discusses topics dealing with becoming a homeowner.

- Industry professionals as guest such as bank underwriters, appraisers, title officers, real estate agents, and mortgage loan officers

- Guest call in number (713) 955-0616

- Shows can be sent by email or SMS to be played later

Other Books by Day Day Publishing

"A Long Road to Redemption Trilogy" is a best-selling action packed urban fiction series. James "JR" Roberts is a successful businessman who has it all. Beautiful family. Successful business. A few bad business deals causes him to lose it all as well as his freedom. Now he finds himself locked up dealing with the demons of his past. This series details the struggles JR has to deal with in order to redeem himself to his family, the business community, but more importantly himself.

Go to <u>www.daydaypublishing.com</u> to order your copies

The McCoy family out of the Virginia Beach area is headed up by the godfather Phillip aka "Big Mack" McCoy. They are the modern day Corleone family. They control all drugs, gambling, prostitution and anything else on the east coast of the country. They also are the largest minority hotel owners in the country. Big Mack has always dreamed of moving his family out of the illegal business and making his family completely legit. His visions the McCoys being just like the Kennedys. The only problem is there are people who will lose a lot if they go legit. This series is full of action, suspense, sex, and excitement.

An urban Christmas tale. Ebenezer Robinson is a successful businessman but unsuccessful in his personal life. He's a mean, selfish, uncaring man who literally hates the holiday season. Ebenezer encounters a little girl who is really sick and in need of help to survive. He's visited by memories of holidays past, present, and future which teach him the true meaning of Christmas.